DISMANTLING
INSTITUTIONAL
WHITENESS

NAVIGATING CAREERS IN HIGHER EDUCATION

The success of diverse faculty entering institutions of higher education is shaped by varying factors at both the individual and institutional levels. Gender, race, class, ethnicity, and immigrant generation as well as their intersections and interplay influence experiences and aspirations of faculty members and administrators. Women have earned half or more of all doctoral degrees for almost a decade yet remain disproportionately underrepresented in tenured and leadership positions throughout academia.

The Navigating Careers in Higher Education series utilizes an intersectional lens to examine and understand how faculty members and administrators navigate careers and their aspirations to succeed. The series includes edited collections and monographs that adopt an interdisciplinary, empirical approach that has theoretical, pedagogical, or policy impacts in addition to enabling individuals to navigate their own careers. Books may adopt a US or a global focus, and topics may include addressing sexism, homophobia, racism, and ethnocentrism; the role of higher education institutions; the effects of growing nontenure-track faculty; the challenge of research agenda that may be perceived as controversial; maintaining a life-work balance; and entering leadership positions. Additional topics related to careers in higher education are also welcome.

Series Editors

Mangala Subramaniam, Series Editor
Professor and Butler Chair and Director, Susan Bulkeley Butler Center
for Leadership Excellence, Purdue University

M. Cristina Alcalde, Series Coeditor
Vice President for Institutional Diversity and Inclusion and Professor,
Global and Intercultural Studies, Miami University

DISMANTLING INSTITUTIONAL WHITENESS

Emerging Forms of Leadership in Higher Education

edited by

M. Cristina Alcalde and Mangala Subramaniam

Purdue University Press · West Lafayette, Indiana

Cataloging-in-Publication Data is on file at the Library of Congress.

978-1-61249-771-6 (hardcover)

978-1-61249-772-3 (paperback)

978-1-61249-773-0 (epub)

978-1-61249-774-7 (epdf)

Cover image: Grafner/iStock via Getty Images

CONTENTS

Acknowledgments　　　　　　　　　　　　　　　　　　　*vii*

Introduction
Gendering and Racializing Contemporary Leadership
in Higher Education　　　　　　　　　　　　　　　　　　**1**
M. CRISTINA ALCALDE AND MANGALA SUBRAMANIAM

1　"As a Campus Community, We Stand With . . ."
Leadership Responsibility in Addressing Racism
on University Campuses　　　　　　　　　　　　　　　**17**
MANGALA SUBRAMANIAM AND ZEBA KOKAN

2　Making Noise and Good, Necessary Trouble
Dilemmas of "Deaning While Black"　　　　　　　　　　**55**
CAROLYN R. HODGES AND OLGA M. WELCH

3　Aligning Narratives, Aligning Priorities
Untangling the Emotional and Administrative Labor
of Advising in Liberal Arts Colleges　　　　　　　　　　**79**
JENNIFER SANTOS ESPERANZA

**4　On the Perils and Opportunities of
Institutionalizing Diversity**
A Collaborative Perspective from Academic Unit-Based
Diversity Officers　　　　　　　　　　　　　　　　　**99**
M. CRISTINA ALCALDE AND CARMEN HENNE-OCHOA

5   *Vale la pena*
    Faculty Leadership and Social Justice in Troubling Times   **131**
    TANYA GONZÁLEZ

6   **Disruptive and Transformational Leadership
    in the Ivory Tower**
    Opportunities for Inclusion, Equity, and
    Institutional Success   **157**
    PAMELA M. LEGGETT-ROBINSON AND
    PAMELA E. SCOTT-JOHNSON

Afterword
    Strategies and Lessons for Changing the Leadership
    Landscape in Higher Education   **187**
    MANGALA SUBRAMANIAM AND M. CRISTINA ALCALDE

    Contributors   *203*
    Index   *209*

ACKNOWLEDGMENTS

The individual conversations about the experiences of women of color in leadership positions in higher education that sparked this collaborative project took place at the 2019–20 HERS Institute, during, after, and in-between sessions. The coeditors not only met each other there but also met many other women in leadership positions across institutions in the United States, including some who later contributed to this project. For that, we are profoundly grateful to the HERS Institute and the space it provided for these conversations and connections, and to our HERS cohort. The conversations we had there and the conversations and experiences we brought from separate institutions all confirmed the need for this volume. Working on this project brought new insights, both about the persistence of challenges to women of color in leadership positions and about the weight of the work done and the structural and systemic work that is still needed in higher education across institutions.

This collection is the first book in the Purdue University Press series, Navigating Careers in Higher Education, launched in May 2020. Justin Race, director of Purdue University Press, was excited and enthusiastic to discuss and finalize the book series when Mangala first approached him. Justin also brilliantly shepherded this book project from initial idea to completed manuscript with care, dedication, and enthusiasm. The editorial board for the series for which this book is a part also engaged with and supported this project, and we thank each editorial board member for that. We also want to thank the two anonymous reviewers who provided valuable feedback on the manuscript, and who did so during a particularly challenging year—both the pandemic and the growing protests for racial justice.

More than anything else, we want to extend our profound gratitude to the contributors to this volume. The conversations and experiences upon which each chapter is built are often left unacknowledged and unanalyzed. Speaking up, talking back, telling our stories, and engaging with research and analysis of these simultaneously deeply personal and professional experiences is not only courageous but also extremely generous, and we recognize and value these efforts. We hope, along with our contributors, that what is in these pages will help both those experiencing what the leaders discuss and those in positions to work alongside women of color leaders to help challenge inequitable, exclusionary systems, structures, and practices.

Cristina also thanks her spouse Joe and sons Santiago and Emilio, her parents Pilar and Xavier, and her siblings Gabriela and Gonzalo for their constant support. The academic leaders and colleagues who worked with her along the way and provided support, encouragement, and, most significantly, friendship, also made this possible and contribute daily to ongoing efforts to make higher ed more just. Thank you, especially, to Monica Diaz, Patricia Ehrkamp, Kathi Kern, Mark Kornbluh, and Huajing Maske. She also wishes to thank Carmen Henne-Ochoa for her friendship, collaborative spirit, and support. At Miami University, she extends a special thank you to president Greg Crawford for his leadership and commitment to efforts and initiatives that embed more inclusive practices to support students, faculty, and staff. Last but by no means least, she thanks Mangala for her friendship, collegiality, and collaborative work. She could not have had a better colleague and coeditor throughout the multiple conversations, plans, and iterations that fueled this deeply personal and professional endeavor.

Mangala is grateful for her inspiring parents, Narayani and P. R. Subramanian, and the tremendous support of family members—Vasanta, Brintha Lakshmi, Shobha, Ravi, and Yogendra. Her entry into university administration about four years back was not planned; it was somewhat of a new experience, and yet it has been very fulfilling despite the challenges. She believes that the initiatives and programs she continues to envision and implement successfully are because of the positive involvement of Purdue's faculty, particularly Purdue's current provost, Jay Akridge. She deeply appreciates his tremendous support. It has been instrumental to initiating and pursuing key initiatives for faculty success from the Susan Bulkeley Butler Center for Leadership Excellence, as well as for opening opportunities for her to grow as a leader. She will remain ever grateful for that. She acknowledges the friendship of faculty colleagues Dulcy Abraham, Linda Mason, Malathi Raghavan, Donna Riley, Aparajita Sagar, Chris Sahley, Stacey Connaughton, and Laura Zanotti particularly for their time and effort, and especially their willingness to discuss and share insights. I appreciate the guidance and realistic advice from my mentor, Teresa Sullivan, president emerita, University of Virginia.

Thanks are due to Zeba Kokan for writing the chapter with Mangala despite the challenges she was facing as she completed her undergraduate studies. She also thanks Lauren Heirty who patiently coded the statements for the data analysis.

Mangala reciprocates Cristina's sentiments about the professional relationship we have built since our first collaborative effort in 2020 and which began with a piece about leadership in *Inside Higher Ed* (July 2020). She has enjoyed the many conversations with Cristina about the challenges in higher education and looks forward to many more. Thanks, Cristina, for serving as a coeditor for the book series as well.

M. Cristina Alcalde and Mangala Subramaniam

INTRODUCTION

Gendering and Racializing Contemporary Leadership in Higher Education

M. CRISTINA ALCALDE AND MANGALA SUBRAMANIAM

W hat does it mean to embody change as a leader of color in a space of normative masculinity and whiteness? Across differences of professional and personal backgrounds, disciplines, administrative roles, and life stories, the narratives and experiences of the women of color in this book foreground that leadership is always already gendered and racialized, and that disrupting long-standing structures and hierarchies carries professional and personal costs. In spite of these costs, women of color leaders engage in transformative and inclusive forms of leadership to bring about change. In our own experiences and those of our contributors, we see a pattern reflected: women of color leaders are increasingly called upon to bring about change to make higher ed institutions more diverse, equitable, and inclusive, even as our presence, actions, and practices are viewed with suspicion and met with resistance in the predominantly white world of higher education. This pattern is not unique to us or our contributors. This book serves as a tool to recognize, analyze, and learn from the microlevel experiences and macrolevel structures in which women of color live and work in higher education in the United States today.

At a time when books such as DiAngelo's *White Fragility*, Kendi's *How to Be an Antiracist*, and Banaji and Greenwald's *Blindspot: Hidden Biases of Good People* underscore the systemic racism in all aspects of everyday life, it is particularly urgent that we consider how women of color leaders in academia both embody change and experience and resist racism and biases in higher education. We are certainly not the first to bring attention to these increasingly urgent topics. Some books discuss leadership and change, such as Kotter's *Leading Change*, Buller's *Change Leadership in Higher Education: A Practical Guide to Academic Transformation,* and Bolman and Gallos's *Reframing Academic Leadership,* yet they do so without sustained attention to the axes of difference—gender, race, ethnicity, and sexual orientation, among others—that circumscribe the everyday lives of leaders in institutions of higher education. Books that do incorporate one or more aspects of difference tend to fall into categories of how-to and guides on the one hand and testimonials on the other hand. These books, from which we and others continue to learn and benefit, include Chun and Evans's *Leading a Diversity Culture Shift in Higher Education: Comprehensive Organizational Learning Strategies,* Williams's *Strategic Diversity Leadership: Activating Change and Transformation in Higher Education,* Chun and Feagin's *Rethinking Diversity Frameworks in Higher Education,* and Stewart and Valian's *An Inclusive Academy: Achieving Diversity and Excellence.*

Ahmed's *On Being Included: Racism and Diversity in Institutional Life* moves away from how-to approaches to provide a broader critique of diversity and the role of racism in higher education yet focuses primarily on the macrolevel and the ways in which institutions work rather than on the experiences and analyses of work within institutions by those in leadership positions. The little attention to women of color *as leaders* in existing books can perhaps be attributed to the lack of such representation in universities (Alcalde and Subramaniam). Although the second volume of *Presumed Incompetent* (Gutiérrez y Muhs) has one short section on leadership, its goal is not to capture the experiences, challenges, and even opportunities for women of color leaders. The first volume of

Presumed Incompetent is a compilation of narratives and testimonials of faculty members' experiences in academia, and therefore, their recommendations and lessons are not specifically about leadership or how to diversify university leadership. Hodges and Welch's *Truth Without Tears: African American Women Deans Share Lessons in Leadership* focuses on women of color leaders, specifically from the perspective of African American women deans. Our book complements this valuable scholarship by foregrounding the leadership experiences of women across multiple personal and professional identity categories at the same time as it provides a unique lens for understanding the *work* of leadership and how women of color navigate university spaces. These experiences, our chapters emphasize, include professional costs and consequences that all too often remain invisible.

Past scholarship that discusses change within organizations assumes institutions comprise rational and objective people without consideration of the gendered and racialized implications of leading for change (cf. Kotter; Buller). However, critical scholars of race, leadership, and higher education consistently show that institutions of higher education are better understood as microcosms of our racialized, gendered, hierarchical society (Chun and Evans; Stewart and Valian). The experience and expertise of African American, Asian American, and Latinx women leaders in these pages push us to engage with the complex decision-making processes, nuances, and everyday forms of resistance from which change in higher education becomes possible. As Hodges and Welch (chapter 2) emphasize, women of color in administration commonly confront the same forms of tokenization, stereotyping, and bias they previously experienced in faculty roles. McKee and Delgado recently collected a series of first-person accounts that foreground how the bias, tokenization, microaggressions, and marginalization that women of color experience as administrators and faculty are also experienced by graduate students of color, pointing to the persistence of early obstacles and challenges women of color experience in higher education. Focusing on graduate education and the experiences of graduate students, Posselt similarly discusses how culture-specific practices and biases work against diversity, inclusion, and change in science, technology, engineering, and mathematics disciplines that pride themselves on objectivity. In short, by the time we become leaders through our administrative roles, many of us have already survived and persisted through our graduate student and faculty experiences, only to find the obstacles to be the same or exacerbated the higher-up the administrative ladder we reach.

Leadership in higher education has increasingly meant leaders approach their universities, and units within (such as departments and colleges), as businesses and bureaucratic, hierarchical organizations. Yet, while the business world grasped the significance of diverse teams for success and innovation decades ago, higher education has been slower to actively seek and accept change. In practice, even the very concept of leadership has long been associated with white, elite masculinity and continues to elevate individualism, competition, and aggression over inclusion and relationality (Liu). This means that efforts to create more inclusive forms of leadership by women of color deans, associate and assistant deans, advising leaders, and others who appear in the following chapters are met with suspicion at best and, most often, by strong overt and covert forms of resistance in response both to the positioning and the practices of these leaders. In this context, talk of diversifying administration and leadership by recruiting and retaining "women and people of color" may be shorthand for white women, who have made more gains than women of color and who far outpace the representation of women of color in faculty and administrative positions. In the following sections, we introduce the main themes across chapters to contribute to our understanding of the experiences and possibilities for women of color leaders for dismantling whiteness in higher education at a time when diversity has become increasingly accepted—if not always operationalized—as a key component of institutional success.

APPROACHING WHITENESS IN ACADEMIA

While women of color are increasingly sought out by recruiters for upper-level administrative roles, those making decisions at the highest levels continue to be predominantly white, and more specifically white men. In 2016, only fourteen percent of administrators in higher education in the United States were racial or ethnic minorities (Seltzer). Today, the landscape continues to be such that women of color work in spaces in which we are often the only nonwhite administrators, and more often the only women of color. This is directly connected to the still-low numbers and underrepresentation of women of color in tenured and full professorships. As Ahmed reminds us, in higher education, approaches to diversity tend to prioritize changing perceptions of whiteness over changing the realities that sustain whiteness and the status quo. In this context, dismantling whiteness can be a lonely uphill battle that the people whose identities have historically been marginalized are, paradoxically, charged with leading.

Throughout this volume, we emphasize the experience of working within the parameters of predominantly white institutions (PWIs) for women of color. We include experiences in large, research-intensive doctoral institutions and small liberal arts colleges. Even as student bodies across higher education become increasingly diverse and historically Black universities and Hispanic-serving institutions thrive, and tribal colleges gain more visibility, it is worth remembering that the colonial university was created to educate the offspring of white colonizers and therefore to preserve racialized and gendered social hierarchies and inequalities (Thelin). Across higher education, the buildings we teach and work in and the residence halls our students live in were built by enslaved Black people on land forcibly taken from the original indigenous inhabitants. Today, those doing the cleaning, cooking, and caring for the buildings and everyday workings of universities continue to overwhelmingly represent minoritized identities, while the highest positions of power (chancellor, president, provost) continue to be predominantly white and masculine.

Women of color faculty and administrators, as the chapters that follow illustrate, continue to be called upon as essential caregivers at the same time as our emotional labor is dismissed as an unwritten part of our leadership roles and embodiment of diversity, and any refusal to provide this additional labor is viewed as defiant or worse. In her leadership role in the area of student advising, Esperanza (chapter 3) examines how the measures used to evaluate the practice of advising miss much of the on-the-ground advising that takes place and the emotional labor that makes successful advising possible in small liberal arts colleges, while Alcalde and Henne-Ochoa (chapter 4) make visible ways in which emotional labor is an unwritten central component of leadership positions in the realm of faculty diversity work.

POSITIONALITY AND REFLEXIVITY

Position and location in terms of gender identity, class, racial and ethnic background, migration status, and different abilities are the basis of the experiences of women of color across layers of leadership. These intersecting identities shape career trajectories, the leadership positions women of color are expected or allowed to inhabit, and the roles they fulfill, which are frequently stereotyped in gendered and racialized ways. The structure of higher education institutions, with a predominantly white leadership at the highest levels, precludes women of color from completely engaging in transformative actions. In that sense, our agency is partial and restricted and in turn influences our sphere of influence and recognition.

Experiences of stereotyping and tokenization are common for women of color. As Esperanza notes in her chapter in this collection, she was often described as *approachable* to students of color, although faculty had not yet come to know her because she was new on campus. She was also being asked to pronounce Chinese names under the assumption that she represents all Asians. Esperanza is a Filipino American woman. These experiences also draw our attention to the lack of understanding of racial and ethnic groups or countries of origin, especially among the dominant white majority. Similarly, Subramaniam and Kokan in their discussion of universities' statements released after George Floyd's death note that the "location and position of who is speaking out loud impact the perception of whether their concerns will be taken seriously by university leadership. At times, there is a double standard for people of color speaking out. If a person of color speaks in a way that may be perceived as 'loud,' they are deemed angry, and the issue may be dismissed" (p. 23). In their contribution to this collection, Hodges and Welch discuss their experiences of "deaning while Black" and being stereotyped and cast into roles not in line with their actions/beliefs. Leggett-Robinson and Scott-Johnson note that they understand the importance of knowing the potential sacrifices of speaking forthrightly. Their critical lens of disruptive leadership is grounded in lived experiences of intersectionality and the impact of the resulting engagements along their career trajectories. González draws on her leadership trajectory to examine how her own positionality as a Latina woman informed both how she experienced her own set of "firsts" and how others perceived her.

The (in)visibility/hypervisibility associated with how women of color leaders are positioned is also reflected on by the chapters in this book, including by Alcalde and Henne-Ochoa, who foreground how even within their specific unit-based leadership roles as diversity workers, they must continuously navigate these extremes as Latinx women. Their roles as leaders in the realm of diversity work foreground that institutionalizing diversity leadership positions does not necessarily mean that the institution is willing to be transformed (Ahmed). Reflecting on their roles, identities, skills, and experiences, Alcalde and Henne-Ochoa remind us that the expertise of women of color leaders does not prevent those same leaders from being labeled as *fiery, aggressive, demanding, headstrong,* or *problematic* as a way to exclude or diminish the power of those leaders.

Like Esperanza and other contributors in this book, for Alcalde and Henne-Ochoa, the racialized and gendered embodiment of women of color leaders also means they are viewed as particularly accessible to others whose identities have been historically marginalized or underrepresented in higher education. Faculty of color are most often the ones who take on the advising of students of color and the mentoring of other faculty of color, and who volunteer for or are appointed to diversity committees (Allen et al.; Cartwright et al.). Thus, it is women of color's embodiment of difference that is interpreted by others in ways that create the conditions and expectations through which women of color leaders are often overburdened by the invisible and unrecognized yet critical labor of supporting—by mentoring, speaking up for—other women and men of color within the institution. While the feeling of satisfaction as a result of following through on commitments of supporting others and contributing to the transformation of structures may be one reward, it is also clear that leaving unrecognized the invisible labor, which many in this volume take on, carries professional and personal costs.

Telling our counterstories of costs, rewards, and tears—as Hodges and Welch, and Esperanza, in particular, encourage us to do—is an important part of both enacting individual forms of reflexivity and of inviting others across higher education to do so to challenge inequitable structures supported by long histories of excluding, or making invisible the labor of, people of color. The contributions in this volume encompass the professional and the personal because, as we emphasize throughout, the boundaries between these two are fluid, and women of color leaders are never simply "leaders." We are always already gendered and racialized, and this phenomenon creates the conditions of tokenization and invisibility/hypervisibility we each analyze and reflect on from our professional, academic, and intimately personal positionalities. As editors, in referring to women of color in this introduction, we intentionally use "their" and "our" interchangeably in referring to the patterns of experience of women of color to signify our own positionalities within this broad category and the pervasive nature of these experiences.

DISRUPTION AND RESISTANCE: ON THE LIVED EXPERIENCE OF DISMANTLING STRUCTURAL WHITENESS

We are profoundly grateful to each of the contributors for sharing their knowledge, expertise, and experiences in the following chapters. We are also aware that there is much that, necessarily, must remain unsaid and unwritten. The personal or professional risks may be too high for the individual or for others, the pain too raw, or the trauma too close. Perhaps one colleague's advice to one of us to wait until after retirement to safely say that which is still silenced can serve as a reminder to readers that what is left unsaid can be as powerful as what is written in these pages. Disrupting and dismantling is not easy work. Sometimes we are the first in our position, as we discuss next, and sometimes we do not have the mentors and colleagues to lean on when we most need it, while other times key factors remain outside of our control.

The lack of diversity in leadership implies that the few women of color moving into administrative positions are often the first in the roles and perhaps "guinea pigs" in a sense. Subramaniam is the first woman of color in the current position that has evolved and changed in terms of expanding support for faculty and even understanding support because of variations in experiences of faculty based on gender, race, and immigrant status. Esperanza is the first Asian American woman to earn tenure at Beloit. Alcalde was the first Latina to hold an associate dean position in her academic unit at her former institution, and is the first Latina to hold her current role. Hodges and Welch were the first African American deans in their institutions. Similarly, González is the first Latina faculty senate president at a Research 1 institution and most recently the chair of the university task force charged with evaluating faculty affairs policy through an anti-racist, social justice lens.

There is additional labor and risk attached to being the "first." Fulfilling the responsibilities involves interfacing with a gendered and racialized face of university administration and specifically the emotional labor that becomes an integral part of the lives of women of color whose performance is closely monitored and critiqued as we are simultaneously made invisible and hypervisible, depending on the circumstances. Dismantling structures of oppression, then, implies a significant investment of emotional labor in efforts to disrupt the status quo. These efforts, perhaps particularly when one is the first, accompany the arduous intellectual and physical work necessary to define a new role, create the infrastructure necessary to support the role and make it meaningful for the individual and institution, and ensure that the work we do is respected and recognized as a way to make the path a bit smoother for other women of color to take on leadership roles and for institutions to become more inclusive in sustainable ways.

Women of color, such as those whose experiences are covered in this collection, often feel isolated, and our work may feel lonely because we don't know who to use as a sounding board or who to trust. While our desires and goals are to be agentic and to aim for the transformation of institutions, we also understand the importance and possible consequences of pushing boundaries. In many situations, when or how we say something is as important as the preliminary decision of whether or not to say it. We may use silence as a way to express disagreement in a way that does not put our careers or those of others at immediate risk, we may use silence as a way to protect ourselves or others from the cumulative effect of microaggressions, and we may use silence to draw attention to a particular issue or question.

BOOK OUTLINE

The chapters that make up this book collectively present and analyze the journeys of transgression, resistance, and bias many women of color leaders confront in the predominantly white realm of higher education in the contemporary United States, particularly in senior leadership positions. While these experiences differ by institution, career trajectory and role, and personal background, together these narratives provide a unique form of engagement, truth telling, and demands, as well as recommendations for change to dismantle the structures that perpetuate inequities. In the first chapter, Subramaniam and Kokan examine higher education institutions as organizations whose formations, hierarchies, and processes are not race-neutral or gender-neutral. Confronting issues of sexism, racism, ethnocentrism, and homophobia has been a challenge for universities. While responses typically wax and wane over time, they are generally reactive rather than proactive. Institutional responses to racial incidents often take the form of statements from university leadership. And that was the case after the death of George Floyd in the summer of 2020. They analyze the statements released by 130 doctoral institutions in the United States by combining a quantitative and qualitative approach. Using a critical lens, they discuss the ways in which racism and violence are addressed; whether and how solidarity (across minority groups) is incorporated; the references to equity, diversity, and equality; and the implications these have for leadership in higher education to transform predominantly white campus spaces. They argue that the statements are "paper trails" that "provide us with useful insights into each institution's stance on how to address inclusionary practices. What is left unsaid in each statement is just as important as what is explicitly stated. The statements indicate not only the sociocultural environment of racial injustice at a university but also provides a snapshot" of university leaders' roles. They argue that leaders adopt the soft path of releasing statements without a vision for change and action. Their discussion also calls for examining and understanding the experiences of women of color across layers of leadership positions, even if not as provosts or presidents. Profound experiential narratives, such as by the contributors to this collection, provide insights into the tremendous efforts to implement and act on diversity, equity, and inclusion for change.

In "Making Noise and Good, Necessary Trouble: Dilemmas of 'Deaning While Black,'" Hodges and Welch draw on their considerable experience as senior administrators and on broader scholarship to address a central dilemma of how to carry out their administrative roles effectively while maintaining integrity and advancing justice in spaces in which, as the first African American deans at each of their institutions, their actions were constantly under scrutiny. Viewed with suspicion yet brought in to enact change, Hodges and Welch examine the various forms of obstacles they confronted and provide suggestions for leadership strategies to contribute to the dismantling of whiteness. Similarly, Leggett-Robinson and Scott-Johnson, as Black women leaders, note that they negotiate the social and political structures. Like Esperanza, Hodges and Welch share their counterstories of pain, struggle, and accomplishments to record their experiences and provide ways for other women of color and institutions to avoid some of the more difficult moments they faced.

In "Aligning Narratives, Aligning Priorities: Untangling the Emotional and Administrative Labor of Advising in Liberal Arts Colleges," Esperanza examines patterns of gendered, racial, and cultural stereotypes at PWIs through a discussion of her experiences in the area of advising. As the first Asian American woman to gain tenure at her institution, she confronted multiple forms of structural violence and microaggressions on her leadership path. From being expected to correctly pronounce all foreign names because of her own perceived foreignness to having her own leadership aspirations suddenly interrupted, the ways in which those in positions of power perceived and approached her identity as a woman of color took a very real toll on her leadership trajectory.

In "On the Perils and Opportunities of Institutionalizing Diversity: A Collaborative Perspective From Academic Unit-Based Diversity Officers," Alcalde and Henne-Ochoa approach diversity work as inherently troublesome and examine challenges faced by unit-based academic diversity leaders. Their chapter complements scholarship on institutional diversity work, which has tended to focus on the role and experiences of chief diversity officers and has neglected the role of unit-based leaders. Like Hodges and Welch, Alcalde and Henne-Ochoa foreground the paradoxical mandate women of color leaders confront; we are formally charged with bringing about change, even as loyalty to long-standing inequitable structures and processes upon which the institution is founded is required. The chapter foregrounds affective labor, the negotiation of invisibility/hypervisibility as Latinx women, and the professional and personal costs of affective and other forms of labor.

Tracing her "unusual" leadership journey, González draws on Ahmed's work to discuss the "scratches" in the walls. Writing on the walls of higher education marks the experiences of those who speak up about inequality on campuses. Ahmed calls these speakers the *misfits* who are called upon to serve institutions in part to avoid major protests, flare-ups, and disruptions on campus. González notes that, whether found in diversity committees of various kinds or affinity group leadership, misfits produce "misfit methods" that are instructive as we lead diversity work from unusual leadership positions. At the same time, González, even in the relative safety of an English department and as someone who also finds an interdisciplinary home in the fields of American ethnic studies and gender, women, and sexuality studies, views herself as participating as a misfit in the work of scholarship, teaching, and engagement within the university community and beyond. She raises critical questions, such as who is scratching the walls? How are these scratches presented? And how do they remain visible for future scratchers? All of this implies that diversity work requires insistence.

Focusing on one path to institutional change, Leggett-Robinson and Scott-Johnson discuss disruptive and transformational leadership. As they note, "Transformational leadership is the ability to articulate a vision and the ability to inspire followers, while disruptive leadership is concerned with the empowerment of others through organizational structures. Thus, to transform, disruption must first occur" (p. 175). The existing majority leadership has been stagnant with ideas, approaches, and solutions regarding these challenges. Black women in leadership have strong (little known) records of unearthing existing systems and structures and replacing them with innovative and effective alternatives. In short, Black women lead from a place of disruption. As Black women, they emphasize that the intersections of gender and race in lived experiences provide the basis for disruptive leadership: "(1) challenge hegemony, (2) include voices from the periphery, and (3) engage in disruptive wonder (question and reassess the social constructs beneath the problem)" (p. 176). Leggett-Robinson and Scott-Johnson discuss tactics that may be used by disruptive Black leaders. They explore the way Black women in leadership negotiate their social structures to disrupt the status quo and implement positive alternatives that better serve the academy and their communities.

In the afterword, we first focus on the lessons learned from the contributors' experiences and strategies that may be useful as women of color leaders navigate the higher education landscape. We also consider why such experiences, with some exceptions, are yet to be integrated theoretically and analytically into scholarship despite the many public pronouncements of "commitments" to diversity made by institutions of higher education. We attribute the lack of integration of experiences, such as those experiences examined in this book, at least partially to the construction of knowledge about leadership by those in dominant/powerful positions and from lenses that are deeply gendered and racialized. Following these lessons, we discuss three overlapping themes that are intertwined in the experiential narratives of the authors: the multiple marginalities experienced in PWIs, doing diversity work, and the responsibility of leaders to frame and take action to foster diversity, equity, and inclusion.

Together, the chapters invite us to examine everyday experiences central to progress, the personal and professional costs of that progress on individual women of color, and the distance still left to travel in making institutions in higher education more diverse, inclusive, and equitable. With each chapter, and cumulatively, we invite readers to envision and support leadership in ways that recognize and allow for learning through the work of women of color who are always already gendered and racialized in the spaces in which we learn, work, live, and lead.

WORKS CITED

Ahmed, Sara. *On Being Included: Racism and Diversity in Institutional Life.* Duke UP, 2012.

Alcalde, Cristina M., and Mangala Subramaniam. "Women in Leadership Positions: Challenges and Recommendations." *Inside Higher Ed*, 17 July 2020, https://www.insidehighered.com/views/2020/07/17/women-leadership -academe-still-face-challenges-structures-systems-and-mind-sets.

Allen, Walter R. "The Black Academic: Faculty Status Among African Americans in U.S. Higher Education." *The Journal of Negro Education*, vol. 69, 2000, pp. 112–27.

Banaji, Mahzarin R., and Anthony G. Greenwald. *Blindspot: Hidden Biases of Good People.* Bantam Books, 2016.

Bolman, Lee G., and Joan V. Gallos. *Reframing Academic Leadership.* Jossey-Bass, 2011.

Buller, Jeffrey L. *Change Leadership in Higher Education: A Practical Guide to Academic Transformation.* John Wiley & Sons, Inc., 2015.

Cartwright, B. Y., et al. "Examining Racial Microaggressions in Rehabilitation Counselor Education." *Rehabilitation Education*, vol. 23, 2009, pp. 171–82.

Chun, Edna, and Alvin Evans. *Leading a Diversity Culture Shift in Higher Education*. Routledge, 2018.

Chun, Edna, and Joe Feagin. *Rethinking Diversity Frameworks in Higher Education*. Routledge, 2020.

DiAngelo, Robin. *White Fragility*. Beacon Press, 2018.

Gutiérrez y Muhs, Gabriella, et al. *Presumed Incompetent: The Intersections of Race and Class for Women in Academia*. UP of Colorado and Utah State UP, 2020.

Hodges, Carolyn, and Olga Welch. *Truth Without Tears: African American Women Deans Share Lessons in Leadership*. Harvard Education Press, 2018.

Kendi, Ibram X. *How to Be an Antiracist*. One World, 2019.

Kotter, John P. *Leading Change*. Harvard Business Review Press, 2012.

Liu, Helena. "Reimagining Ethical Leadership as a Relational, Contextual and Political Practice." *Leadership*, vol. 13, no. 3, 2017, pp. 343–67.

McKee, Kimberly D., and Denise A. Delgado, editors. *Degrees of Difference: Reflections of Women of Color on Graduate School*. U of Illinois P, 2020.

Posselt, Julie R. *Equity in Science: Representation, Culture, and the Dynamics of Change in Graduate Education*. Stanford UP, 2020.

Seltzer, Rick. "Failing to Keep Up." *Inside Higher Ed*, 2 Mar. 2017.

Stewart, Abigail, and Virginia Valian. *An Inclusive Academy: Achieving Diversity and Excellence*. MIT Press, 2018.

Thelin, John. *A History of American Higher Education*. Johns Hopkins UP, 2004.

Williams, Damon A. *Strategic Diversity Leadership: Activating Change and Transformation in Higher Education*. Stylus, 2013.

1

"AS A CAMPUS COMMUNITY, WE STAND WITH . . ."

Leadership Responsibility in Addressing Racism on University Campuses

MANGALA SUBRAMANIAM AND ZEBA KOKAN

As a campus community, we stand with the family of Ahmaud Arbery, who was murdered while jogging in Georgia by two white men. We stand with Christian Cooper, who was the victim of a woman's attempt to use the police as a weapon against him while he pursued his passion for birdwatching in New York's Central Park. We stand with the loved ones of Breonna Taylor, an essential worker during this pandemic who was killed in her home by police. We stand against the senseless killing of George Floyd in Minneapolis by a police officer who knelt on his neck, while three others watched and assisted, as Mr. Floyd choked out the same final words of another slain Black man, Eric Garner: "I can't breathe."

— UNIVERSITY OF CALIFORNIA, BERKELEY

The above quote is drawn from the statement released by the leaders of the University of California, Berkeley, following the death of George Floyd in the summer of 2020. The statement brings together a myriad of racial injustices and conveys the significance of racial oppression and the violence that occurred. It is a call to protest the systemic racism we encounter. The explicit linking of examples of injustices to Black bodies emphasizes the dire need to call upon institutional leaders to recognize the weight of their words and the absence of their actions.

Two crises challenged institutions of higher education in 2020: the devastating effects of COVID-19, including the racism faced by Asian Americans and disproportionate impacts on Black Americans, and the racial injustices amplified by the death of George Floyd. Floyd was killed on May 25, 2020, while in police custody in Minneapolis, sparking nationwide protests and calls for the end of police violence against Black citizens. This death, as well as countless before this and those that have occurred since May 2020, draw attention to the discrimination and inequalities that are based in race and ethnicity, as well as other forms of difference. These differences are about how power is structured and configured. The protests have spilled into educational institutions, and many universities responded with statements from leaders.

Higher education institutions are organizations whose formations, hierarchies, and processes are not race-neutral (Ray) or gender-neutral. In fact, issues of sexism, racism, ethnocentrism, and homophobia are not new to institutions of higher education. Confronting them has been the challenge; responses typically wax and wane over time but are generally reactive rather than proactive. Moreover, inadequate funding and the lack of justice frameworks for implementation are common within higher education. Institutional responses to selective or major, not all, incidents of racism have typically been in the form of statements from university leadership. And that was the case after the death of George Floyd in the summer of 2020. What do these statements put out by universities convey? Do they describe actions taken/to be taken and how? What are the implications of the findings for leadership in institutions of higher education? How can leaders be attentive to diversity, equity, equality, and inclusion based on "difference" and the intersections of differences (race/

ethnicity, class, and immigrant status-foreign-born and first-generation immigrants) that are structured as relations of power and privilege? We address these questions by discussing the findings from the analysis of the statements released by 130 doctoral institutions in the United States. Whether and how statements from university leadership will begin or continue a process of institutional transformation is debatable. We argue that the statements provide us with useful insights into each institution's stance on how to address inclusionary practices. What is left unsaid in each statement is just as important as what is explicitly stated. The statements indicate not only the sociocultural environment of racial injustice at a university but also provide a snapshot into the institutional structure.

Using a critical lens, we combine a quantitative and qualitative approach to analyze the statements. We examined the ways in which racism and violence are addressed; whether and how solidarity (across minority groups) is incorporated; the references to equity, diversity, and equality; and the implications these have for leadership in higher education to change predominantly white campus spaces. We note how the language may be co-opted without clear gains in change or without consideration of continuous investments by recognizing there is no "quick fix." As a foreign-born immigrant and a first-generation Asian American, respectively, we (the authors) reflect on our positionality at a major doctoral institution and so also draw on our experiences in explaining the findings and recommending strategic action.

FRAMEWORK: UNIVERSITY LEADERS AND STATEMENTS ABOUT RACISM

University leaders are important administrators who are responsible for addressing gendered and racialized incidents on campuses. Cole demonstrates how academic leaders in the mid-twentieth century were a driving force behind many social changes as they actively, although often quietly, shaped policies and practices, both inside and outside of the educational sphere. Notably, presidents developed multicampus university systems to streamline college access, dismantled the original higher education affirmative action programs, and leveraged Confederate imagery—three actions linked to contemporary racial struggles. Unfortunately, in contemporary times, university leaders have been reactive and rarely "walk the talk." University leaders respond to incidents as a one-time event as opposed to the result of the systemic racism embedded within institutions of higher education. They fail to place their money where their mouths are, leading to empty promises and abandoned task forces.

Racialization within institutions must also contend with the unmarked whiteness of higher education leadership. Critical race theorists consider whiteness a form of property: a resource encompassing "all of a person's legal rights" (Harris 279). At the same time, the concept of "white institutional space" provides a broader frame for thinking about how the unmarked whiteness of organizations shapes agency (Moore 27). Three of Moore's descriptive elements of white institutional space—racialized exclusion, racial symbolism, and the normative elements of white institutions—underly our analysis of statements. Statements that condemn racial incidents rarely name the targets and may through diversity programs reinforce and legitimate racial hierarchies they are purportedly designed to undermine. Additionally, people of color, by conforming to racialized organizational scripts, can often reproduce structures of inequality that may prevent alliances across minority groups. Therefore, the lack of accountability within statements and the masquerading of people of color, unconsciously or consciously, advance the "white institutional space" and cultivate a poor environment for transformative change.

We use the arguments made by Tamtik and Guenter and draw on the lens of critical policy studies in education (Ball, *Politics* and "What Is Policy"; Henry et al.; Ozga) to note that statements are not only texts or documents but reflect social relationships, power, and institutional responsibility to transform experiences of those who are different. The content of the statements, as well as who puts them out and what "educational values" have been endorsed or explained, is key to understanding the institutions' intent. In fact, they are more than "texts" and related to power and authority "leading to local interpretations of equity, diversity and inclusion" (Tamtik and Guenter 44).

University statements become "paper trails" and often are commitments (Ahmed 17). How we read these commitments and what such commitments do matters. For example, "a commitment to antiracism in referring to racism is what an institution is 'against' could even be used to block the recognition of racism within institutions" (Ahmed 16). Thus, it is perhaps not surprising that despite institutional rhetoric that highlights the importance of diversity, Ahmed argues that institutions themselves can be primary sources of resistance to diversity work and structural change.

Statements cannot fix diversity, address racism, alter campus climate, or provide knowledge about these topics. However, statements are starting points to actionable change; the absence of any statement may be a form of resistance to diversity work by refusing to acknowledge an equity gap within an academic institution. Efforts to institutionalize diversity and inclusion goals are certain to face resistance (Ahmed), and without the ability and capacity to build relationships and convince key stakeholders to engage in the change process, leaders will likely be unsuccessful (Harvey; Wilson). Getting these constituents involved and interested in diversity work is not without challenges, but it is crucial because organizational change requires collaboration, buy-in, and a collective institutional vision and commitment (Kezar).

One challenge arises from leaders tending to use the term *diversity* in narrow binary terms that often starkly contrast Black and white and marginalize all other racial and ethnic groups, resulting in the exclusion of some minoritized groups. The convenience of viewing, referencing, and responding in binary notions of race and skin color fail to consider the multiracial forms of difference and shades of skin color (Glenn;

Subramaniam, "Underpinnings of Gender"). Binary thinking has consequences for articulating and enabling change. First, it pushes the unreferenced categories of racial and ethnic groups even further to the margins, enabling a sense of divisiveness and competition for resources and attention (see, for instance, Kang). And this may be further exacerbated by the predominantly white leadership, as well as people of color in positions of power. Faculty of color, with diminished capacity and power, are compelled to relish the marginal spaces from which "to see and create, to imagine alternatives, new worlds" (hooks 150). Although the faculty of color in positions of power are usually a minority, their visibility as people of color can cause complacency in their white colleagues who mistake their presence in that space as proof of having solved problems of institutional equity. Therefore, when criticism on the effectiveness of existing approaches to diversity and inclusion are highlighted—some people of color are met with dismissive tones.

Second, the approach stifles and precludes or limits the creation of alliances to demand change by recognizing commonalities and differences. Huynh, in a recent article, calls for Asian Americans to support Black Lives Matter. She notes, "In response to this, Asian Americans need to shred the model minority myth because it has been weaponized and used as a tool to uphold White supremacy because of our proximity to Whiteness. If we are complicit or stay silent, we continue to make it harder for other marginalized groups to exist, survive, and thrive in America." Despite the different histories of the various racial/ethnic groups, and even generationally, the experiences of racism, including microaggressions, are not uncommon (cf. Chun and Feagin; Lui; Sagar). Consider, for instance, the limited spaces within which the racism faced by Asian Americans in the wake of COVID-19 was acknowledged. While it was widely covered in the press, there was little to no proactive effort by universities to express support for Asian Americans on campuses. So oftentimes, racism is not even "named." Third, adopting a binary lens in considering racial categories undermines intersectional experiences, such as the intersections with gender and class.

Circling back to the point of leadership, it is important to note that up to this point, changes in the structure in higher education key leadership roles have been all too slow; they lag far behind demographic changes. At the same time, the kind of diversity work that is valued is closely tied to who speaks the loudest and not about who has the knowledge and vision for change. Moreover, the location and position of who is speaking out loud impact the perception of whether their concerns will be taken seriously by university leadership. At times, there is also a double standard for people of color speaking out loud. If a person of color speaks in a way that may be perceived as "loud," they are deemed angry, and the issue may be dismissed.

Focusing on the complexities of naming racism, the need for enabling alliances and building solidarity across racial and ethnic groups, and the understanding of diversity, inclusion, and equity, we argue that university leaders adopt the soft path of releasing statements without a vision for change.

STATEMENTS AND POSITIONALITY OF AUTHORS

Our data comprise the statements of 130 Research 1 universities following the brutal killing of George Floyd in the summer of 2020. These statements were compiled from online sources. See Appendix A for the list of statements. We combine a quantitative and qualitative approach to examine the statements. For the quantitative analysis, we created a coding rubric, tested it, and then each of the authors independently coded the statements for twenty variables. For this chapter, we use selected variables that address the three themes we examine in the following sections: mention of racism and the targeted group, solidarity, and whether equity, diversity, and equality are mentioned. The qualitative component entailed a grounded theory approach to make meaning of the quantitative coding. Both, the creation of the coding schema and the qualitative analysis are also influenced by our (authors) own position and location in academia and in society.

The first author (Subramaniam) is a foreign-born South Asian immigrant. She pursued higher education in the United States and started as a tenure-track assistant professor at her current institution. She moved up the ranks to become a full professor and was appointed to her current position in the same institution. As a faculty member of color and as a social scientist, she has pursued scholarship in the area of social inequality particularly gender and its intersections with race, caste, and class. This knowledge has shaped many of the initiatives she has created for faculty in her current role in the administration. In her administrative position, she focuses on professional development offerings, mainly for faculty, and in doing so, she recognizes how axes of "difference" circumscribe the everyday lives of faculty and institutional structures. She is neither an insider nor an outsider.

A researcher who shares the same gender, racial, ethnic, and social-class background as her/his subjects is considered to be an "insider" with them, while one whose status characteristics differ from those of her subjects is considered an "outsider" (Baca Zinn; Merton). Scholars who critique the dichotomous notions of insider and outsider argue that ethnic outsiders are very capable of studying those of classes and ethnicity/race different from their own. They justify this with the positivist argument that an "objective" social scientist can be "neutral" (e.g., "professional") in research and analysis (cf. Horowitz; Sanchez-Jankowski). It is important to note that when "whiteness" studies "whiteness," questions of objectivity and neutrality are rarely called into question. But this is not the same for minority groups.

Some positivists might even argue that only an outsider can be sufficiently detached to research and write scientifically about what they see, study, and describe. In sociology, some white men and women have produced insightful studies of groups whose class and/or ethnicity/race are not the same as their own (cf. Bourgois; Miller; Stack; White). We argue that one way to breach the insider-outsider log jam is to see interactions and structures as dynamic and multiple rather than—as often presented in methodological texts and in some academic discussions—as role-set static opposites. Such dynamics may be based on the position and role we, authors, occupy within an institution of higher education.

Despite being in the current role for a little over three years now, she (Subramaniam) describes herself as an outsider within—demographically—and in the structure of leadership.[1] She has frequently felt like an outsider or a "space-invader" to use Puwar's term. While Puwar emphasizes skin color, we integrate gender and note that invading spaces is also about being a foreign-born immigrant and a woman of color in the university administrative structure.[2] From the current vantage and unique position, she (Subramaniam) is attentive to diversity and inclusion while being focused on faculty needs for success. This work has involved enormous emotional and intellectual labor that cannot be tangibly measured and so is rarely rewarded.

Yet she has developed initiatives and programs that have been contributing to the success of faculty. She is able to do the work because of the enormous support that has come from allies and specific individuals in positions of authority. It has required much resilience on her part, which most faculty who compliment the efforts of the Susan Bulkeley Butler Center for Leadership Excellence are probably unaware of. Without the support, she wonders if she would have remained in this or any administrative leadership position. She notes this knowing full well that it conveys her vulnerability and tentativeness. The supportive upper leadership also made it possible for her to work with an accomplished woman leader, outside of the institution, as her mentor. These aspects were instrumental in building her confidence, developing resilience to pushbacks and challenges, and creating innovative programs and initiatives.

The second author (Kokan) is an undergraduate student. She is a first-generation South Asian American raised by Indian (South Asian) immigrants. She approaches scholarship and community engagement through an interdisciplinary lens. She is invested in issues of diversity and inclusion and involved in various related forums and committees. Kokan has been attentive to the social and spiritual needs of Muslims on campus and promotes community, civic, and service engagement, considering she is a Muslim. Kokan's experience with how other people view her ethnicity, nationality, religion, and gender has often been reduced to the sum of its parts instead of being seen in totality. This oversimplification of identity has strengthened her view on the importance of intersectionality.

She (Kokan) strives to work at the intersection of global affairs, public health, and the social sciences. As a 2020 Truman Scholar, she has been committed to using her platform to uplift the voices and stories of those underrepresented in public discourse. She is an insider to the student experience and has a firsthand feel of what it means to be a person of color attending a Research 1 institution. While being an American citizen provides her increased access to understanding cultural and language norms, she can be an outsider in predominantly white spaces. She is an insider to the experiences of people of color but an outsider to the Black experience. As an undergraduate student, she does not fully comprehend the bureaucracy of higher education, as she is primarily in classroom and campus settings. This differs from the experiences of the first author (Subramaniam) who navigates both worlds—academia and administration.

Both authors, as persons of color, are deeply invested in the transformation of academic spaces that will allow those like us, and those different from us, to not only survive but also thrive in academia. As people of color, our experiences intersect with knowledge as deeply tied to issues of diversity, inclusion, equity, and equality. We are outsiders in different ways—our status within the university, a faculty member and administrator versus an undergraduate student. In acknowledging how we are positioned, we believe that this study of university leaders' statements on racial incidents can contribute to starting an important dialogue, developing constructive action, becoming cognizant of processes, and implementing action for combating racism on campuses.

PROFILE OF STATEMENTS

We coded each of the 130 statements using the rubric we developed.[3] Each of the authors coded the first ten statements to test for reliability and then coded twenty statements with the revised codes independently. This iterative process allowed us to fine-tune and develop a robust set of codes for the variables and the basis for the data we used for the quantitative analysis. For the qualitative analysis, we began with an initial read of the statements and then reread them closely and marked them for topics of interest—references to racism and the targeted group, solidarity, and whether equity, diversity, and equality are mentioned. These topics were gleaned in a close reading of each university statement by the second author. Our analysis draws from the quotes in the extensive notes created from the statements.

University leaders, typically at the level of the dean and above, released the university statements. While seventy-nine of the statements bore the name of the president or chancellor of the university, four were by the provost alone, and six bore the names of both the president and provost of the university. About thirty-two percent (n = 41) of the statements were released by multiple university leaders, conveying a sense of cohesive response. See table 1.1. While sixty-six percent of the statements were released by male leaders, fourteen percent were released by female leaders, and twenty-three percent had names of both male and female leaders (sig, $p < 0.0001$).[4] The statements varied in length from 85 words to 1,560 words (excluding the title and signature line). We turn now to discuss the content of the statements.

TABLE 1.1 Author of Statement

UNIVERSITY LEADER	NUMBER (%)
President	79 (60.8)
Provost	4 (3.1)
President and provost	6 (4.6)
Other	41 (31.5)
Total	*130 (100)*

WHAT DO THE STATEMENTS CONVEY?

As discussed previously, we examined the ways in which racism and violence are addressed; whether and how solidarity is incorporated; the references to equity, diversity, and equality; and the implications these have for leadership in higher education.

Addressing the Targeted: Racism and Violence

Racism—a word that has divided our country and our world for decades. As we've watched the nation's events unfold in the recent wrongful death of George Floyd, our hearts are deeply grieved. So many in our country are asking the important question, "What can we do?"

— UNIVERSITY OF TENNESSEE

About seventy-eight percent of the institutions allude to racism (table 1.2) like the University of Tennessee, but only about thirty-one percent refer to systemic or institutional racism. For instance, Case Western Reserve University notes, "But what about the systemic racism cited so often in recent days? How can a city, a country, 'clean up' that? We cannot—should not—ever try to wipe away the past. We need to know it. Own it. And commit to forging a better future." Similarly, Cornell University asserted, "While the challenges are enormous, and we cannot fix them on our own, that does not absolve us from taking whatever

TABLE 1.2 Referencing Racism

MENTIONS	NUMBER (%)
Racism	101 (77.7)
Any type of racism	45 (34.6)
Systemic/structural/institutional structural/embedded racism	40 (30.8)
Individual racism	2 (1.5)
Systemic/institutional/structural/embedded racism/individual racism	2 (1.5)
Anti-Black racism	1 (0.8)

steps we can to fight against systemic racism and structural inequality." And, the president of Colorado State University was emphatic: "We are committed to being anti-hate, anti-bias, and anti-racist."

However, almost 21% of statements reference no target group (see table 1.3). While 36.2% of statements explicitly reference Blacks and/or African Americans as targets, an additional 3.8% mention Blacks and/or African Americans with other racial/ethnic groups, such as Latinx and Asian Americans. Interestingly, although Black Lives Matter (BLM) protests were significant soon after the death of Floyd, 93% of the statements do not mention BLM. Additionally, the name George Floyd is not mentioned in about 11% of the statements.

TABLE 1.3 Specific Racial Categories

CATEGORY	NUMBER (%)
None mentioned	27 (20.8)
Black and/or African American	47 (36.2)
Black and/or African American and Latinx and Asian American	5 (3.8)
People of color or minority communities	13 (10.0)
Asian	1 (0.8)
Other	37 (28.5)

Some institutional statements, like that of the New Jersey Institute of Technology, convey introspection by asking questions about diversity and biases.

> Have we challenged racism and ignorance, even when we see it expressed subtly in "polite company" by those we would consider to be colleagues or friends? Have we honestly questioned and explored our own biases and how they shape our behaviors? Have we worked hard enough to create diversity, and with it greater understanding of and appreciation for one another, throughout our networks and organizations? Have we been guilty of, despite our best intentions, moving on to the next crisis of the day and failing in our commitment to make positive change?

In contrast, some universities, like Oregon State University, call out the failed "justice system" but do not discuss the actions or policies of their own institution.

Our findings are similar to Cole and Harper's study of selected statements released by university presidents in the wake of racial incidents. Most offer a vague explanation, and some do not acknowledge the targeted groups. Only a few or none situate their responses to racial incidents within the larger historical context that fosters racial hostility on many college campuses. In fact, each racial incident is spoken of as a one-time occurrence. One may ask, What about references to other minority groups in the statements? Such references can be aimed at building alliances across minority groups to bolster demands and action to address racism. We turn to this aspect next.

Alliances and Solidarity

Building alliances across minoritized groups can be crucial for addressing racism. Race-/ethnicity-related talks between groups of color, especially when addressing personal and group experiences of racism, may be prone to the "who's the more oppressed" trap (Sue, *Overcoming Our*

Racism, Race Talk). There is little doubt that each group, whether Native American, African American, Latina/o, or Asian American can claim that it has suffered immensely from racism. So, using one group's oppression to negate another group's is to diminish, dismiss, or negate the claims of another (Sue, *Race Talk* 170). The failure to bridge differences and understand one another is damaging and serves to separate rather than unify.

Acknowledging the differences in histories and the impact of stereotyping, and at the same time being attentive to the commonalities, can be fruitful for change. As Huynh notes,

> Our collective liberation and destinies are intrinsically interconnected with other communities of color; especially the Black community as history revealed that the Civil Rights Movement in the 1960s was a pivotal turning point in ending the race-based immigration quota system, which benefited numerous Asian immigrants. Our fight for equality and racial justice is a marathon—not a sprint—and requires a consistent commitment to being anti-racist or else we'll continue to be used as pawns to systematically uphold White supremacy.

As noted earlier, 79% of the statements reference a target group. About 3.8% mention Black and/or African American with other racial/ethnic groups, such as Latinx and Asian American (refer to table 1.4). Almost 61% of statements do not mention other minority groups in shared solidarity, but about 27% of the statements use the terms, "people of color, communities of color, minority communities or indigenous" (see table 1.4). For instance, the Duke University statement notes,

> Every day, throughout our country, African American and other marginalized communities have their safety and dignity threatened—in their places of work, in public spaces, and in their homes and neighborhoods. This ongoing history of structural and sustained racism is a fundamental and deeply distressing injustice, here as elsewhere.

TABLE 1.4 Other Groups Mentioned in Shared Solidarity

GROUPS MENTIONED	NUMBER (%)
None mentioned	79 (60.8)
People of color, communities of color, and minority communities, indigenous	35 (27)
Indigenous	2 (1.5)
Low-income	2 (1.5)
Other	12 (9.2)

Other institutions, such as Kansas State University and Massachusetts Institute of Technology (MIT), reference prejudice across racial/ethnic groups and indirectly acknowledge the racism they faced.

> At the start of the COVID-19 pandemic, around the country, we witnessed acts of prejudice toward those from China and other Asian countries. Now, we are witnessing protests over the killing of black and Latino individuals by law enforcement officers. This is clearly no time to be silent on issues of social justice. (Kansas State University)

> I know that the pain of these events is especially intense for certain members of our community, beginning with those who are African American and of African descent, though certainly not ending there. And I know that, in this time of tension around the pandemic and rising strains in US-China relations, others in our community are also suffering distinctive forms of harassment and discrimination. (MIT)

Justice, being an ally, or solidarity is referenced in about twenty-five percent of the university statements. Racial justice and/or social justice are alluded to in about twelve percent of the statements, and economic justice, along with racial and social justice, is included in just two statements (see table 1.5).

For instance, the statement from the Georgia Institute of Technology says, "I acknowledge the pain many members of our community are

TABLE 1.5 Words of Affirmation of Justice

AFFIRMATION OF JUSTICE	NUMBER (%)
No mention	63 (48.5)
Racial justice and/or social justice	16 (12.3)
Solidarity or ally	13 (10)
Social justice and economic justice and racial justice	2 (1.5)
Ally and social justice	1 (0.8)
Other	35 (26.9)

feeling, and I stand in solidarity with our African American brothers and sisters and all people of goodwill, as we find a path forward."

However, less than ten percent of statements mention gender, and so they fail to capture the intersectional nature of life experiences. Among the exceptions is the University of California, Berkeley, statement, which states, "Less noticed by the mainstream media but equally important to elevate are Black women, gender non-conforming and trans people who have been murdered in recent weeks and months." Yet almost ninety percent of statements include some mention of oppression in the form of one of the following phrases: *racism, hatred, discrimination, intolerance,* and *systemic discrimination/oppression.*

The mixed bag of sentiments expressed in the university statements fails to emphasize the structurally and institutionally pervasive racism—overt and covert. Despite this, whether the statements reference and consider diversity, equity, and inclusion is what we turn to next.

Diversity, Equity, and Inclusion

Incorporating key terms such as *diversity, equity, equality,* and *inclusion* would be strategic on the part of universities, even if it is mere posturing. But the strategic nature of using these words creates a campus environment where *diversity* and *inclusion* are buzzwords. Some administrators use it to signal a level of sophistication or progressiveness, without actually doing the labor needed for transformation within an organization. It is insufficient to prop up equity affirmations without walking the walk.

TABLE 1.6 References Diversity, Equity, Inclusion, Equality, Multiculturalism

REFERENCES	NUMBER (%)
Not mentioned	39 (30.0)
Diversity and/or inclusion and/or equity and/or equality	76 (58.5)
Other	15 (11.5)

While thirty percent of the statements include no such terms, more than half (about fifty-eight percent) of the statements reference some combination of these phrases: *diversity*, *equity*, *equality*, and *inclusion*. Among those that do not reference diversity, equity, or inclusion are Auburn University, Boston University, Boston College, Columbia University, and Harvard University. Several universities, including Emory University, Brown University, and University of Mississippi, incorporate these phrases in their statements (see table 1.6).

For example, the Brown University statement states,

We are a community that does not condone acts of racism, discrimination or violence. This cannot be accepted as "normal." We must continue to demand equity and justice for all people, inclusive of all identities. And we must continue to care for and support each other, especially in this time when we are apart.

Universities such as Princeton and the City University of New York (CUNY) Graduate Center relate equity concerns to their mission. The following quote from the CUNY statement is an example:

CUNY and The Graduate Center have a firm policy on equal opportunity and non-discrimination, which states, "Diversity, inclusion, and an environment free from discrimination are central to the mission of the University." We remain committed to that policy and to carrying it out in all of our actions.

At the same time, some universities noted their failure to address diversity, equity, and inclusion and acknowledge that they can do more. Consider for instance the acknowledgments in the Brandeis University and Carnegie Mellon University statements.

> Our university was founded on principles of inclusion that are as relevant today as they were in 1948. As I said at the community virtual gathering last week, we have not always lived up to our ideals, but those ideals—our values—point us in the right direction. The administration and I are committed to moving beyond "business as usual" and requesting voluntary efforts for change. We must work together to build a community that is diverse, welcoming, and free from bias and discrimination. (Brandeis University)

> At times like this we must reflect on what we can do to make society, including our own community, more just. It would be inadequate to restate our commitment to respect, value, and foster diversity, equity and inclusion across our community. We know we have much work to do to live out these values at Carnegie Mellon. Learning about each other's lived experiences; engaging with and supporting colleagues; challenging injustice when we witness it; and, especially, actively listening to each other will truly help us build the campus climate we seek. (Carnegie Mellon University)

Many institutions' statements emphasize students rather than all campus constituencies. In doing so, they overlook the importance and need for diverse faculty as critical for student retention and as role models for students. For instance, the Georgia Institute of Technology notes that the institution has recently worked on a "new vision of inclusion, public, service, and impact" with emphasis on students rather than all campus constituencies. Similarly, the Princeton University statement asserts, "I ask all of us to join the graduates in the Class of 2020 in their quest to form a better society, one that confronts racism honestly and strives relentlessly for equality and justice." It would be pertinent to note here that a very long list of demands for support was made by faculty, staff, and administrators following George Floyd's death and the anti-racism protests.[5] The "Faculty Letter" noted that the demands were on behalf of "Black, Latinx, Asian, and members of all communities of color along with our white colleagues," clearly pointing to an alliance of multiple minoritized and privileged groups.

It is ironic that despite decades of concerns with equity in higher education institutions, evident in scholarly work and in the content of course offerings, statements of universities seem to reference it as if it were a relatively new concern. The statements do not include what actions, if any, would be needed to address equity. University leaders may also delegate the responsibility for addressing these concerns to diversity offices, which has both positive and negative implications. On a positive note, such delegation acknowledges the expertise of those in diversity offices, but at the other end, it also negates the importance of the issue, as it is not addressed by institutional leadership at the helm of the university. Additionally, some like Iowa State University reference diversity, equity, and inclusion in the context of the local campus police without connecting it to the campus and academic culture as a whole. Such "police-centric" assertions raise concerns about how institutions of higher education will determine what to do about ensuring equity.

DISCUSSION AND CONCLUSION: ROLE OF UNIVERSITY LEADERSHIP

In this chapter, we examined the 130 doctoral institutions statements released by universities after the death of George Floyd in the summer of 2020, focusing specifically on three key themes: the ways in which racism and violence are addressed, whether and how solidarity is incorporated, and the references to equity, diversity, and equality. Based on the analysis we consider the implications these have for the leadership in higher education to change predominantly white campus spaces. From our different and yet similar vantage points—student versus faculty member and administrator but both as people of color keen on institutional change beyond rhetoric—we interpret our findings in the context of leadership.

Statements are "paper trails" that are neither policy nor are they put into practice or required to be acted upon. And, for the most part, they are similar to campuses addressing the racial crisis with an appropriate response of writing a report with a set of recommendations (Kezar and Fries-Britt). More importantly, being proactive in addressing gender and racial/ethnic inequities and allocating resources for constructive action is far more significant than reactive statements. The act of releasing statements is often described as conveying commitment, but there is a lack of specificity in what forms of action can be expected by whom and when or the ability to hold accountable those in major leadership positions. Moreover, if the commitment is not to address the underlying and systemic inequities, then it is performative, like the celebration of diversity being about having different cuisines or dressing in varying national costumes. It emphasizes diversity as being "happy talk" (Bell and Hartmann).

Our findings show that leaders rarely reference the targeted groups and incidents pertaining to racial violence. The typical response to the incident is to handle it as a sole event with no connection to past incidents and the specific targets. Universities tend to respond to racial incidents as "teaching moments," which is certainly needed, but it is a problem in that it ends there without the much needed action or steps to move forward by leadership. Therefore, university leaders fail as role models when their responses are programmed, such as in the form of a statement without mentioning the targets and remaining silent on concrete steps for change.

Anger, distrust, fear, and fatigue are the primary areas that campuses need to address after a racial crisis (Kezar and Fries-Britt). Campuses could struggle to address these primary areas without role models among leaders. Leaders have the influence to shape policies and practices and therefore they are role models for how to develop and act on a diversity, inclusion, and equity agenda. As pointed out by Cole, "The views of the president—whose voice is arguably seen as a proxy for the stance of the university—are critical to showing that institutions' leaders will not tolerate racism" (20).

While not directly evident in our analysis of statements, one way that institutions respond to racial incidents is to create a committee or task force. Such a routinized approach to racial issues on campus rarely creates change and will be particularly weak in addressing the trauma created by a racial crisis (Kezar and Fries-Britt). Yet committees and task forces are created as a panacea to address racism, but they are formed with little transparency. Oftentimes, the "usual suspects" are tapped and included, which is a sign of institutionalized racism (Hughes). And then there is the uncertainty regarding the content of the report. As noted by Kezar and Fries-Britt, most campuses will approach racial crisis with an inappropriate response of writing a report with a set of recommendations. Inappropriate because it neither provides the time nor space for addressing the traumatic experiences nor to begin laying out action for constructive change. Such action must be transparent, including inbuilt accountability parameters, particularly for those in leadership positions.

Additionally, Selzer and colleagues write forcefully about acknowledging white racial privilege along with socioeconomic status. Taking responsibility could perhaps include organizing a panel session about white privilege (Selzer et al.), which is as much needed as is one about race and racism. This is much needed especially because those who hold positional power and status are more likely to be white and/or cisgender men, who may have little experience with reflecting on their own power and privilege (Harvey).

Not naming the target or referencing other groups can also be detrimental to building networks of solidarity for change. Alliance across racial and ethnic groups is the second theme we examined. As we noted, more than half of the statements do not mention any other racial or ethnic group or, more broadly, people of color. It is, no doubt, important to name a targeted group and equally significant to reference other minority groups to facilitate alliances and building solidarity networks to mitigate isolation and prevent fractures. This has implications for inclusive excellence and the responsibility of leadership to recognize differences (such as varying histories) and at the same time build on commonalities (racism and macroaggressions they encounter). Such solidarity networks are critical for addressing isolation and sharing concerns and successes. Any effort to elevate any one single group alone can lead to discussions about "who is more oppressed" (Sue, *Overcoming Our Racism*, *Race Talk*), which can be divisive and preclude the inclusion of diverse voices for change. Additionally, solidarity efforts are key for the retention of faculty of color and must be recognized by leaders. There is a need for more "disruptive" leadership (Leggett-Robinson and Scott-Johnson).

In our own experiences, there are tensions and contradictions about how racism is understood within various layers of the institution, particularly when university leaders fail to act to transparently create and put in place specific measures to address racism faced by marginalized groups. To reiterate, leaders whose actions related to addressing racism are not transparent and without built-in accountability are unlikely to bring about change in institutions of higher education. This also draws our attention to the minimal diversity at top levels of university leadership (cf. Alcalde and Subramaniam). Universities that emphasize recruiting and diversifying the student body rarely reference that for faculty and leadership by, say, allocating resources for major cluster hires targeting diversity. Opportunity hiring (diversity related) is a strategy, yet those hires can be isolated in units. These concerns are also directly related to the third theme we examined—diversity, equality, equity, and inclusion.

It is unclear if institutions understand the terms *diversity*, *equity*, and *inclusion*. In fact, scholars note that there is much variation in terms of how equity is defined (cf. Tamtik and Guenter). For instance, equity can be addressed as fairness versus equity as inclusion. Equity as inclusion allows for organizations to change so that all individuals can achieve the basic minimum, while equity as fairness allows for changes that can potentially secure the maximum success for equity-seeking groups (Clarke). Lack of specificity has a direct effect on creating policies, actions, and implementation. In our analysis of statements, most leaders reference diversity, equity, inclusion, equality in terms of binary notions of race and color that fail to capture the growing multiracial population in the United States across the shades of skin color (cf. Glenn; Subramaniam, "Underpinnings of Gender").

Mainstreaming diversity is needed, but that can result in people without power in positions of authority who may be compelled to comply with leadership strategies and thereby alter the agenda and action. In her candid and astute analysis of the dilemma of Black women academics at predominantly white institutions, "Why I Clap Back Against Racist Trolls Who Attack Black Women Academics," Stacey Patton notes,

> Universities want to create the illusion of diversity and to profit from that illusion, but they are showing little interest in making campus classrooms and curricula more inclusive, more welcoming, more honest, more intellectually rigorous. Once Faculty of Color are inside the building, once Students of Color pay their tuition and have their picture taken for the university website, all bets are off. The message we receive is clear: We got you for what we need, now sit down, shut up, and be counted for our diversity report while we pat ourselves on the back and call it "progress." (338)

There is a trend to use positive university-backed data on diversity and inclusion to shut down conversations about issues of inclusion. For instance, institutions assert, "our data shows otherwise," which is used to negate the experiences of people of color, especially that of Black women.

Leaders can recognize, reward, and amplify diversity work and at the same time ensure that action is congruent and cohesive across layers of the university. The responsibility to steward campuses through racial crises falls on leaders but as suggested by Kezar and Fries-Britt, they must aim at building capacity to handle and recover from a racial crisis.

> Campuses will be better prepared if they provide strategic leadership to build capacity and resiliency for diversity, equity, and inclusion initiatives over time. Capacity building means that an investment is made by the campus to regularly assess the preparedness of the campus and to identify the gaps in resources, services, and knowledge, so that leaders have the skills needed to work with communities. The investment in capacity building is not a static process and should not be approached with a check the box-one-and-done attitude. DEI work is ongoing, multifaceted, complex, and always changing. Leaders must keep a pulse on the day-to-day realities of the campus to detect problems before they become a crisis. They understand the sustained nature of DEI work and the need to remain invested, even when things appear to be "improving." (Kezar and Fries-Britt)

Such capacity building is essential for all leaders and should include experiential (such as case-based) discussions of intersections of gender and other forms of differences. Providing resources to enable such education would be meaningful (cf. Subramaniam et al. *Best Practices Tool #4A, Best Practices Tool #4B*).

Being involved in campus-related diversity, equity, and inclusion initiatives at different levels, we as authors, have experienced attempts to temper the ways we display our involvement so that we do not tilt the institution's agenda to shift the status quo for change. Any attempts to act for inclusion, beyond the performative, that do not allow the continuance of the inequitable processes and policies are viewed as "extreme." Our experiences reinforce the often acknowledged note about the challenges in changing institutional structures, which are described as "banging your head against a brick wall" (Ahmed 26). Institutional leaders may interrupt diversity and inclusion work based on their perception that these efforts are in conflict or are less important than other institutional goals, like preserving institutional excellence and prestige or free speech (Ahmed). The fact that these goals are viewed as being in opposition to diversity and inclusion are forms of structural racism, maintaining existing hierarchies, and systems of power within the academy.

Finally, we acknowledge the limitations of our data, as they rely only on publicly released statements. Although the statements provide us insights into what leaders emphasize or do not say, these written texts are, we believe, paper trails that are less likely to alter relations of power and privilege. Future research should consider examining the processes of how the statements come to be, what policies follow the statements, and how they are implemented.

Most importantly, as we do in this book, it would be meaningful to examine and understand the experiences of women of color across layers of leadership positions, even if not as provosts or presidents. These profound experiential narratives provide insights into the tremendous efforts to implement and act on diversity, equity, and inclusion, but as noted by Esperanza (forthcoming) oftentimes, women of color are compelled to deploy silence strategically in these struggles and also use it as a tool of resistance (see also Aiston and Fo). Despite providing experiential narratives, women of color in leadership positions are asked to provide evidence for racism and inequities. It becomes the word of the woman of color leader versus that of the institution (represented by men and women).

APPENDIX: LIST OF STATEMENTS

Addressing Institutional Racism Now. The Ohio State University. June 10, 2020.

Addressing Intolerance in Our Community. The University of Central Florida. June 4, 2020.

Addressing Racism. Temple University. June 7, 2020.

All University Message. The University of New Mexico. May 30, 2020.

A Message from @LSUpresident. Louisiana State University. May 29, 2020.

A Message from ASU President Michael Crow. Arizona State University. June 1, 2020.

A Message from Campus Leaders: Standing Together. UC Berkley. May 29, 2020.

A Message from Chancellor Yang. UC Santa Barbara. May 29, 2020.

A Message from MSU President Mark Keenum. Mississippi State University. May 31, 2020.

A Message from NJIT President Bloom. New Jersey Institute of Technology. June 1, 2020.

A Message from NYU President Andrew Hamilton. New York University. May 31, 2020.

A Message from Penn State President Eric J. Barron. Pennsylvania State University. June 10, 2020.

A Message from President Becker on Racism and Violence. Georgia State University. May 31, 2020.

A Message President Bob Caslen. The University of South Carolina. May 31, 2020.

A Message from President Fuchs. The University of Florida. May 29, 2020.

A Message from President Harvey Stenger. Binghamton University. May 30, 2020.

A Message from President John Thrasher: An Update to the Campus Community. Florida State University. June 3, 2020.

A Message from President Julio Frenk. The University of Miami. May 31, 2020.

A Message from President Schapiro Regarding the Tragic Events in Minneapolis. Northwestern University. May 29, 2020.

A Message from Provost Wendell Pritchett on the Campaign for Community. The University of Pennsylvania. June 8, 2020.

A Message from Rev. John I. Jenkins, C.S.C.—"We Have Work to Do." The University of Notre Dame. June 8, 2020.

A Message from the Interim President. Graduate Center, The City University of New York. May 29, 2020.

A Message from the President. Tulane University. June 1, 2020.

A message from UI Leaders on Next Steps Following George Floyd Demonstrations. The University of Iowa. June 5, 2020.

A Message on Recent National Events. The University of Mississippi. May 31, 2020.

A Message to Black Faculty, Staff and Students. UC San Diego. June 5, 2020.

A Message to the UTA Community. The University of Texas at Arlington. June 2, 2020.

A Message to Our Aggie Community. Texas A&M University. June 1, 2020.

A Message to Our Community. The University of Wisconsin–Madison. May 31, 2020.

A Message to Our Students as We Near the Close of Spring 2020. UC Davis. June 4, 2020.

A Statement from President Bendapudi: Diversity and Inclusion, Our Cardinal Principle. The University of Louisville. June 1, 2020.

A Message of Solidarity from UNLV President Marta Meana. The University of Nevada, Las Vegas. May 31, 2020.

A Statement on IU's Commitment to Diversity and Equity. Indiana University. May 31, 2020.

An Important Message from President Steven Currall and Dr. Haywood Brown. The University of South Florida. June 8, 2020.

At This Painful Moment. Montana State University. June 2, 2021.

Auburn University President Commits to Changes in the Wake of George Floyd's Death. Auburn University. June 5, 2020.

Boston College Office of the President. Boston College. June 2, 2020.

Breonna Taylor, Our Community and Our Next Steps. The University of Kentucky. June 3, 2020.

Campus Email on the Tragic Death of George Floyd. Stony Brook University. June 2, 2020.

Campus Update. University at Albany State University of New York. June 1, 2020.

Chancellor's Update: A Time for Change. University of Wisconsin, Milwaukee. June 3, 2020.

Comment on the Current State of our Nation: The Work That Remains. Purdue University. June 2020.

Coming Together as a Community. The University of Minnesota. Undated.

Community Message on Racial Injustice. Tufts University. May 31, 2020.

Confronting Racism. Georgetown University. May 31, 2020.

Confronting Racial Injustice. Stanford University. May 29, 2020.

Confronting Racial Injustice. The University of Houston. June 10, 2020.

Confronting Racism in Our Society. Carnegie Mellon University. May 30, 2020.

Constructive Conversations for Societal Change. The University of Michigan. June 5, 2020.

CSU Condemns Floyd Killing, Stands with Community Against Hate and Violence. Colorado State University. May 29, 2020.

During This Time, We Are Here for You. The University of Utah. Undated.

Email to Campus Community: A Message from Chancellor Subbaswamy About Current Events. The University of Massachusetts. May 29, 2020.

Everyone Has a Role to Play. The University of Arkansas. Undated.

Executive Office of the President. The University of Arizona. Undated.

Finding Hope During Difficult Times. Dartmouth University. May 31, 2020.

Following Up on Monday's Letter to the Community. Boston University. June 3, 2020.

From the Chancellor—Standing Against Hate and Violence. The University of Colorado Boulder. May 29, 2020.

From the President's Desk. Rensselaer Polytechnic Institute. Undated.

Gee Calls on Higher Ed to Create Necessary Dialogues, Asks WVU Community to Lean on Mountaineer Values in Wake of Floyd, 'Countless' Other Black Deaths. West Virginia University. June 3, 2020.

Grief, Anger and Needed Change. North Carolina State University. Undated.

I Can't Breathe—Again. The University of Nevada, Reno. May 30, 2020.

Important Message from UAB Leaders. The University of Alabama at Birmingham. June 1, 2020.

In Memory of George Floyd. Yale University. May 31, 2020.

In Support of the African American Community. UC Irvine. May 31, 2020.

Iowa State University Office of the President. Iowa State University. May 29, 2020.

Johns Hopkins Stands in Solidarity Against Racism and Inequity. John Hopkins University. May 31, 2020.

Joint Message from Anne Holton and Greg Washington. George Mason University. June 1, 2020.

Letter from Brown's Senior Leaders: Confronting Racial Injustice. Brown University. May 30, 2020.

Letters to the MIT Community. Massachusetts Institute of Technology. May 29, 2020.

Letters to the UMB Community. Statement on the Death of George Floyd. University of Maryland, Baltimore. May 29, 2020.

Lifting the Veil: Understanding the Clarity This Moment Offers. The University of Washington. May 30, 2020.

Looking Backward, Looking Forward. The University of Virginia. June 3, 2020.

May 29, 2020: Message to the Campus Community on the Shocking Events in Minnesota.

Michigan State University. May 29, 2020.

Message: A Message to the KU Community. The University of Kansas. June 2, 2020.

Message from Campus Leaders on events in Minneapolis. The University of North Caroline at Chapel Hill. May 30, 2020.

Message from President and Provost on Racial Injustice. The University of Connecticut. May 31, 2020.

Message from President Claire E. Sterk. Emory University. May 30, 2020.

Message from President Lee C. Bollinger. Columbia University. June 1, 2020.

Message from President Thomas LeBlanc. George Washington University. May 31, 2020.

Message from Sarah Mangelsdorf and Mercedes Ramirez Fernandez. The University of Rochester. May 30, 2020.

Message from the President to USM Students. The University of Southern Mississippi. May 31, 2020.

Message to Our Community. Syracuse University. May 30, 2020.

Message to the Rice Community. Rice University. May 30, 2020.

Message to the UIC Community. The University of Illinois at Chicago. May 29, 2020.

Message from UGA President Jere Morehead: Planning for Return to Campus. The University of Georgia. April 29, 2020.

Minneapolis, Louisville, Atlanta. University at Buffalo. May 30, 2020.

Note to Community from President Folt. The University of Southern California. May 31, 2020.

No Tolerance for Discrimination and Violence. The University of Missouri. May 28, 2020.

Now Must Be Different. The University of Nebraska. June 5, 2020.

Office of the President. Wayne State University. N.D.

On Racial Equity and Justice. Washington University in St. Louis. May 31, 2020.

OSU President Ray Addresses George Floyd Killing, Riots. Oregon State University. June 1, 2020.

Our Community and Events in Minneapolis and Chicago. The University of Chicago. May 30, 2020.

President Hargis Issues Statement Promoting Respect, Equality and Leadership. Oklahoma State University. June 3, 2020.

President Jere Morehead's Letter. The University of Georgia. June 1, 2020.

President Pinto's Message: The Time to Act Is Now. The University of Cincinnati. June 3, 2020.

President, Provost Call for Focus on Core Values in Wake of George Floyd's Death Minneapolis. The University of New Hampshire. June 1, 2020.

President Pollack Announces Immediate Actions to Support and Strengthen Our Community. Cornell University. June 3, 2020.

President Rosenberg: "We Stand on the Side of Justice and Accountability." Florida International University. May 30, 2020.

President Schovanec Message on Tragic Event in Minneapolis. Texas Tech University. June 5, 2020.

President Snyder and Provost Vinson Issued a Statement Last Night About Local Protests Following the Death of George Floyd. Case Western Reserve University. June 1, 2020.

Racism and Intolerance Have No Place in Our Society. Clemson University. June 1, 2020.

Recent Tragedies a Call for Self-Examination. Washington State University. Undated.

Reflecting on the Events in Minneapolis and Beyond. The University of Illinois at Urbana-Champaign. May 30, 2020.

Responding to the Death of George Floyd. California Institute of Technology. May 30, 2020.

Rutgers Responds to Racial Injustice. Rutgers University–New Brunswick. June 1, 2020.

Speaking Out Against Hatred, Racism and Violence. The University of Oregon. May 29, 2020.

Statement from President Eisgruber on the Killing of George Floyd and the Importance of Confronting Racism. Princeton University. June 1, 2020.

Statement from President Kennedy on the Tragic Death of George Floyd. The University of Colorado. May 31, 2020.

Statement from UTEP President Heather Wilson. University of Texas–El Paso. June 2, 2020.

Statement on Racial Injustice and the Death of George Floyd. The University of Pittsburgh. June 2, 2020.

Statement on George Floyd. Georgia Institute of Technology. May 31, 2020.

Statement on George Floyd. UC Santa Cruz. May 29, 2020.

Statement Regarding Richmond Protests and VCU's Shared Community. Virginia Commonwealth University. May 31, 2020.

Statement to the Community Regarding Minneapolis. Duke University. May 30, 2020.

Steps Toward Greater Justice and Healing. Drexel University. June 3, 2020.

The Fierce Urgency of Now. Northeastern University. June 3, 2020.

The Pain Behind the Protests. UCLA. May 30, 2020.

The University of Oklahoma Office of the President. The University of Oklahoma. May 31, 2020.

Transforming Our Campus to Eliminate Systemic Bias. Brandeis University. June 9, 2020.

Turbulent and Difficult Times. The University of Texas at Austin. June 1, 2020.

UA Community Response to Recent Tragedies. The University of Alabama. May 31, 2020.

UC Riverside Mourns the Death of George Floyd. UC Riverside. May 29, 2020.

UH President Reflects on a Week That Has Rocked Our Nation. The University of Hawai'i at Manoa. June 1, 2020.

University of Delaware. The University of Delaware. June 4, 2020.

University of Texas at Dallas from the Office of the President. The University of Texas at Dallas. May 31, 2020.

University Statement on Social Injustice. Kansas State University. May 29, 2020.

UT Can Be a Beacon of Light. The University of Tennessee. June 1, 2020.

Vanderbilt Statement on Racial Injustice in Our Society (from Interim Chancellor and Provost). Vanderbilt University. May 31, 2020.

We Must Stand Together—An Official Notice from the President. The University of North Texas. June 1, 2020.

What I Believe. Harvard University. May 30, 2020.

NOTES

1. I have made every effort to pursue the mission of the Center and made it a central transformative unit on campus. I can do the work because of the enormous support that has come from specific faculty members and especially those in positions of authority. It has required much resilience on my part, which most faculty who compliment the efforts of the Center are probably unaware of. Without the support, I doubt I would have lasted beyond a semester. I note this knowing full well that it conveys my vulnerability and tentativeness.

2. Puwar (2004) describes how white bodies become somatic norms within spaces and how nonwhite bodies can feel "out of place" within those spaces.

3. The codebook is available from the authors.

4. Bivariate analysis of statement author and gender gives $\chi^2 = 45.558$; statistically significant at $p < 0.0001$.

5. See https://docs.google.com/forms/d/e/1FAIpQLSfPmfeDKBi25_7rUTK khZ3cyMICQicp05ReVaeBpEdYUCkyIA/viewform.

WORKS CITED

Ahmed, Sara. *On Being Included: Racism and Diversity in Institutional Life.* Duke UP, 2012.

Aiston, Sara J., and Chee K. Fo. "The Silence/ing of Academic Women." *Gender and Education*, vol. 33, no. 2, 2021, pp. 138–55.

Alcalde, Cristina M., and Mangala Subramaniam. "Women in Leadership Positions: Challenges and Recommendations." *Inside Higher Ed*, 17 July 2020, https://www.insidehighered.com/views/2020/07/17/women-leadership -academe-still-face-challenges-structures-systems-and-mind-sets.

Baca Zinn, Maxine. "Field Research in Minority Communities: Ethical, Methodological, and Political Observations by an Insider." *Social Problems*, vol. 27, no. 2, 1979, pp. 209–19.

Ball, Stephen J. *Politics and Policy-Making in Education.* Routledge, 1990.

— — —. "What Is Policy? Texts, Trajectories and Toolboxes." *Discourse*, vol. 13, no. 2, 1993, pp. 10–17.

Bell, Joyce M., and Douglas Hartmann. "Diversity in Everyday Discourse: The Cultural Ambiguities and Consequences of 'Happy Talk.'" *American Sociological Review*, vol. 72, 2007, pp. 895–914.

Bourgois, P. "Conjugated Oppression: Class and Ethnicity Among Guaymi and Kuna Banana Workers." *American Ethnologist*, vol. 15, 1988, pp. 328–48.

Chun, Edna B., and Joe R. Feagin. *Rethinking Diversity Frameworks in Higher Education.* Routledge, 2020.

Clarke, M. "The Sublime Objects of Education Policy: Quality, Equity and Ideology." *Discourse: Studies in the Cultural Politics of Education*, vol. 35, no. 4, 2014, pp. 584–98.

Cole, Eddie R. *The Campus Color Line: College Presidents and the Struggle for Black Freedom.* Princeton UP, 2020.

Cole, Eddie R., and Shaun R. Harper. "Race and Rhetoric: An Analysis of College Presidents' Statements on Campus Racial Incidents." *Journal of Diversity in Higher Education*, vol. 10, no. 4, 2017, pp. 318–33.

Glenn, Evelyn Nakano. *Shades of Difference: Why Skin Color Matters.* Stanford UP, 2009.

Harris, Cheryl I. "Whiteness as Property." *Critical Race Theory: The Key Writings That Formed the Movement*, edited by K. W. Crenshaw et al., The New Press, 1995, pp. 276–91.

Harvey, W. B. "Chief Diversity Officers and the Wonderful World of Academe." *Journal of Diversity in Higher Education*, vol. 7, no. 2, 2014, pp. 92–100.

Henry, Miriam, et al. *Educational Policy and the Politics of Change*. Routledge, 2013.

hooks, bell. *Yearning: Race, Gender, and Cultural Politics*. South End Press, 1990.

Horowitz, Ruth. *Honor and the American Dream: Culture and Identity in a Chicano Community*. Rutgers UP, 1983.

Hughes, Robin L. "10 Signs of Institutionalized Racism." diverseeducation.com /article/64583/. Accessed 13 July 2020.

Huynh, Steffi. "Calling Asian Americans to Action: Why We Can't Stay Silent About Black Lives Matter." *Diverse Issues in Higher Education*, 20 July 2020, https://diverseeducation.com/article/184543/.

Kang, Jay Caspian. "We Need to Put a Name to This Violence." *The New York Times*, 6 Mar. 2021, https://www.nytimes.com/2021/03/06/opinion/asian-american -violence-race.html?action=click&module=Opinion&pgtype=Homepage.

Kezar, Adrianna. *How Colleges Change: Understanding, Leading, and Enacting Change*. Routledge, 2014.

Kezar, Adrianna, and Sharon Fries-Britt. "Navigating a Campus Racial Crisis: Building Capacity, Leading Through Trauma and the Recovery Process." *Change: The Magazine of Higher Learning*, vol. 52, no. 2, 2020, pp. 89–93.

Leggett-Robinson, Pamela, and Pamela E. Scott-Johnson. "Disruptive and Transformative Leadership in the Ivory Tower: Opportunities for Inclusion, Equity, and Institutional Success." *Dismantling Institutional Whiteness: Emerging Forms of Leadership in Higher Education*, edited by M. Cristina Alcalde and Mangala Subramaniam, Purdue UP, 2023.

Lui, Priscilla. "When We Understand Microaggressions in the Broader Context of Systemic Racism, We'll Make Some Progress. *Diverse Issues in Higher Education*, 21 Dec. 2020, https://diverseeducation.com/article/199752/.

Merton, Robert. "Insiders and Outsiders: A Chapter in the History of the Sociology of Knowledge." *American Journal of Sociology*, vol. 78, no. 1, 1972, pp. 9–47.

Miller, Eleanor. *Street Woman*. Temple UP, 1986.

Moore, Wendy L. *Reproducing Racism: White Space, Elite Law Schools, and Racial Inequality*. Rowman & Littlefield, 2008.

Ozga, J. *Policy Research in Educational Settings: Contested Terrain*. Open UP, 2000.

Patton, Stacey. "Why I Clap Back Against Racist Trolls Who Attack Black Women Academics." *Presumed Incompetent II*, edited by Yolanda Flores Niemann et al., UP of Colorado, 2020, pp. 332–40.

Puwar, Nirmal. *Space Invaders: Race, Gender and Bodies Out of Place*. Berg, 2004.

Ray, Victor. "A Theory of Racialized Organizations." *American Sociological Review*, vol. 84, no. 1, 2019, pp. 26–53.

Sagar, Aparajita. "Institutional Climates and Women Faculty of Color: Overcoming Aversive Racism and Microaggresssions in the Academy." *Susan Bulkeley Butler Center for Leadership Excellence and ADVANCE Working Paper Series*, vol. 2, no. 2, 2019, pp. 4–15.

Sanchez-Jankowski, Martin. *Islands in the Street: Gangs and American Urban Life*. U of California P, 1991.

Stack, Carol B. *All Our Kin: Strategies for Survival in a Black Community*. Basic Books, 1983.

Subramaniam, Mangala. "Underpinnings of Gender and Colorism in the Culture of Niceness in Universities." *Butler Center and Purdue-ADVANCE Working Paper Series—Navigating Careers in the Academy: Gender, Race, and Class*, vol. 1, no. 2, 2019, pp. 5–16.

Subramaniam, Mangala, et al. *How to Engage in Discussions of Differences Such as Race. Best Practices Tool #4A*. Susan Bulkeley Butler Center for Leadership Excellence, Purdue U, 2021.

— — —. *How to Engage in Discussions of Differences Such as Race. Best Practices Tool #4B*. Susan Bulkeley Butler Center for Leadership Excellence, Purdue U, 2021.

Sue, Derald W. *Overcoming Our Racism: The Journey to Liberation*. Jossey-Bass, 2003.

— — —. *Race Talk and the Conspiracy of Silence: Understanding and Facilitating Difficult Dialogues*. John Wiley & Sons, 2015.

Tamtik, Merli, and Melissa Guenter. "Policy Analysis of Equity, Diversity and Inclusion Strategies in Canadian Universities—How Far Have We Come?" *Canadian Journal of Higher Education*, vol. 49, no. 3, 2019, pp. 41–56.

White, William F. *Street Corner Society: The Social Structure of an Italian Slum.* 4th ed., U of Chicago P, 1993.

Wilson, Jeffery L. "Emerging Trend: The Chief Diversity Officer Phenomenon Within Higher Education." *Journal of Negro Education*, vol. 82, no. 4, 2013, pp. 433–45.

2

MAKING NOISE AND GOOD, NECESSARY TROUBLE

Dilemmas of "Deaning While Black"

CAROLYN R. HODGES AND OLGA M. WELCH

The late Congressman John Lewis implored the nation to "make some noise and get in good, necessary trouble" for the cause of racial justice and equality. His statement and lifelong commitment captured for us the challenge we faced as the first Black deans in the history of our respective units at predominantly white institutions (PWIs)—namely, how to enact our roles responsibly and effectively while retaining our identities and integrity. We both had become full professors and served as department heads at the same university before moving into higher administration. We took on deanships at different universities within two years of each other, with one serving as vice provost and dean of the Graduate School at a large public, very high research university and the other as dean of the School of Education at a private, Catholic high research university. Yet in carrying out our charge as deans, we witnessed and experienced how some of the hurdles that we cleared on our academic journey to the full professorship were present in different forms at executive levels of leadership, where the framework of institutional whiteness posed challenges for "deaning while Black."

INSTITUTIONAL WHITENESS AND
HIGHER EDUCATION

More than three decades ago, Derrick Bell referred to racism and the struggle for racial justice as "unfinished business," describing it as "America's continuing commitment to white domination" (4). Today, racial and gender hierarchies continue to exist within the culture of the academy in the United States and to exert an inequitable, differential impact on people of color. Those hierarchies, created by white males and driven by what arguably can be characterized as a plantation mentality, are supported within a framework that exhibits characteristics of white supremacy culture—that is, a culture of power that discriminates, fosters inequities, and minoritizes based on race. While these characteristics were prevalent and clearly codified in the origins of US educational policies for admissions and hiring, their subsequent invalidation by civil rights legislation did not remove the mindset that still clings to the original structure in somewhat tempered but equally insidious ways and supports ongoing racial inequities within the academy.

Faculty, students, and administrators of color have progressed from being unequivocally excluded from PWIs to having a presence where they are often a small fraction of the student body, and the campus leadership celebrates their presence and heritage as proof of commitment to equal opportunity. Strategies that have been implemented to address this issue have focused primarily on students and, to a lesser extent, on faculty; they include affirmative action admissions and financial support; enhanced academic programming in area studies on women, gender, and race; campus programs for first-generation students; grants to broaden participation in graduate education; and targeted hiring for underrepresented faculty whose portfolios bring diverse perspectives to campus curricula and academic research.

While strides have been made in the educational attainment of students of color in higher education since the changes ushered in by the landmark 1954 *Brown v. the Board of Education* ruling, the American Council on Education disclosed in its 2019 status report on race and ethnicity in higher education that the stark changes between 1997 and 2017 in demographic trends toward a rapidly increasing nonwhite population have not removed substantial disparities by race and ethnicity; among all adults aged twenty-five and older earning bachelor's degrees in 2017, 15.3% were Black, 12.2% were Hispanic, and 23.7% were white. Additionally, educational attainment of students at the doctoral degree level in 2017 shows that 1.1% were Black, 0.7% Hispanic, and 2.0% white (Espinosa et al. 3, 8). The small numbers at the graduate level have an impact on the hiring and retention of faculty of color, which, in turn, has fueled the racial gap in key academic leadership positions at PWIs and created what is referred to in one study as "the enduring whiteness of educational professionals," which has been slow to change (Whitford).

A 2017 research brief by the College and University Professional Association for Human Resources reports that eighty-six percent of administrators in higher education were white and seven percent Black, equal to approximately one-half the percentage of Black students who attained college degrees in 2017 (Seltzer). White men and white women far outpace the representation of women and men of color in faculty and administrative positions, with women of color being least represented. Evidence of strategies to enhance and sustain racial representation in higher education by addressing institutional whiteness has not been broadly discussed. Though representation is changing, the small numbers are indicative of national data, which reflect notable growth in positions focusing specifically on chief diversity officers and staff, who are charged with what often turns out to be the single unrealistic charge of removing any suggestion of an unwelcome campus climate and transforming the institution's image to one that embraces diversity and inclusion. Changes in racial representation exhibit less obvious advancement in upper-level academic appointments, such as deans, provosts, and presidents. More important than following the disparity in numbers in racial representation, however, is studying what happens once a person of color takes on the role of a key administrator and understanding what strategies are in place to enhance and sustain racial representation in higher education leadership.

The struggle to redress inequities in numbers and reduce the racial gap is ongoing and important to address, but it is not enough to change the demographics in higher education administration by adding one or two faces that alter the diversity without transforming the way in which the institutional whiteness veils systemic racism. Sara Ahmed reminds us that diversity cannot be simply about making a change in the "perceptions of whiteness"—that is, moving from a visibly and overwhelmingly monocultural makeup to one that is multicultural but must instead seek to change or dismantle the "whiteness of organizations"—that is, the internal mindset, which—whether unwittingly or by design—presumes superiority, fails to recognize and denies the presence of systemic racism, and expects unquestioning commitment to the status quo (34).

Changes in diverse senior leadership in higher education at many PWIs have revealed advances made through the increase of numbers of white females. While white females have been able to shatter the proverbial glass ceiling, a number of them continue to be treated as interlopers, leaving them to tiptoe around that broken glass—that is, around outdated patriarchal attitudes that constantly remind them that they are displaced and have damaged a status quo believed to be irreplaceable. Black women, on the other hand, who move into leadership positions and break the glass ceiling are considerably fewer in number and are faced with another ceiling, or barrier, if you will, represented by the artificial barrier of color, which enters the white space and influences their white colleagues' and supervisors' perceptions of and interactions with them. We refer to it as an artificial barrier because we, as women "deaning while Black," only became aware of the barrier based on their responses to us. Our new faces of leadership brought a profile and disposition very different from all who preceded us in our roles, and unlike the stereotypes we were imagined to be or into which we were sometimes cast. We were hired presumably as agents of change, but our style of leading was perceived as disrupting the status quo and threatening to the comfortable frame of whiteness of our counterparts. Our actions, which conveyed our clear intention of transforming the status quo in a way that enhanced the operation of our units and fostered a strong commitment to social justice, were met in several ways with resistance and reticence but failed in diminishing our sense of agency and empowerment.

DEANING WHILE BLACK:
HOW DOES IT FEEL TO BE A PROBLEM?

In *The Souls of Black Folk*, W.E.B. Du Bois's seminal work of 1903 on racial inequality and social reform, the author poses the unspoken but implied question on the minds of those in the white world that surrounded him—namely, "How does it feel to be a problem?" (2). It is the beginning of his famous discourse on the color line as the big problem of the twentieth century and introduces his well-known musings on the concept of double-consciousness. Du Bois indicates that he did not see himself as a problem until those moments when he was made to feel so by his white counterparts because of looking different and performing better than expected—generally exceeding expectations. He goes on to offer a very telling description of feeling as if he were born with a veil that symbolizes the feeling of "double-consciousness," which was aroused in the face of racial injustice and evoked a "sense of always looking at one's self through the eyes of others.... One ever feels his twoness ... two souls, two thoughts, two unreconciled strivings; two warring ideals in one dark body, whose dogged strength alone keeps it from being torn asunder" (3). This was a prophetic observation of what was to come in the battles for social justice that were fought throughout the twentieth century and which remain at the crux of twenty-first-century pleas to counter enduring whiteness by moving beyond passive tolerance to active anti-racism.

As Black female deans, we faced a conundrum; that is, on the one hand, we were hired to transform our units—in one case, to rebuild a graduate school and strengthen the profile of and output in graduate education for the campus, and in the other case, to secure national accreditation in teacher education and heighten national visibility of all undergraduate and graduate programs in the School of Education. On the other hand, we were frustrated by a racial and gender hierarchy that threatened to stifle our ability to be the change agents ostensibly desired. While we were the first Black female leaders in our units as models of diversity in action, our commitment to transformation and a renewed vision was in a vulnerable position when confronted with that ceiling or veil Du Bois described, which would suddenly appear and be lowered in response to our proposals and actions. Often, that veil manifested itself whenever we met resistance or silence in response to our plans.

There would be, for instance, unclarified resistance from our immediate superiors to implementing new programs or adding positions for which we had been able to budget in the absence of one-time or limited recurring funding for which many units competed. In another example, after deans learned that it was necessary to produce revenue-building ideas for new initiatives, we suddenly found out that, for unexplained reasons, we would not have control over that revenue. There was a lack of understanding or unwillingness to accept new initiatives related to the uniqueness of our units that called for measures different from those implemented generally across the student body. It could mean a difference in how a unit admitted or dismissed students, for instance, with the implementation of a new student management system. Too many times our arguments were ignored in favor of a one-size-fits-all approach, only to have to be revisited and changed when our warnings proved to be true. Our reporting staff members were also susceptible to a way of thinking that seemed to rely on "how we have always done it." At first, they acted as gatekeepers of information, guarding information they were not ready to share but held for their purposes or because they thought it would trouble us. We learned to circumvent the gatekeeping by "maintaining a policy that invited feedback, even from those we either suspected or knew opposed us, and encouraged a discourse based on free exchange of ideas" (Hodges and Welch 23). Over time, we were able to build general acceptance of our voices of authority as reliable and final.

We had difficulty understanding the source of the resistance at all levels, which felt like mistrust, primarily because of the reticence and unwillingness to discuss our projects. For instance, we prepared carefully for meetings with our superiors only to find ourselves having a one-sided conversation, giving a report, as it were, to which there was little meaningful response, regardless of the questions we posed. That was probably more frustrating than anything else because it happened not only in regular one-on-one meetings but also in annual performance reviews and sometimes in larger cabinet-level meetings. In extreme cases, we would suddenly find out about a decision concerning our unit that had been made without our input and which did not take into consideration the considerable amount of work we had been charged to complete as a part of the university strategic planning. The resistance we faced among some of the staff who reported to us came from those who had been associated with the unit long before our arrival; they were very guarded about information we needed to solve problems and to move forward and instead often sought guidance from other white staff members and administrators in other units whom they knew well. It took a great deal of trust-building, listening, and one-on-one and group staff discussions to adjust the climate and dynamic that would boost unit teamwork and foster loyalty.

Other particularly troubling forms of resistance and reticence manifested themselves in discussions on diversity, in particular, how to address the lack of diversity in a given discipline or improve outcomes for university recruitment initiatives. When we were in such meetings, those leading the discussions did not consult us about how we had done this within our own units, something we dutifully reported in our regular meetings and annual performance reviews. Instead, it often occurred that the discussion about diversity would quickly devolve to discussions on female representation, while attention to recruiting people of color faded because it was the proverbial "elephant in the room" that no one wanted to address. At that point, the conversation became solely focused on recruiting women. The words *race* and *ethnicity* were not part of the conversation and strategies for retention were abandoned, if mentioned at all, and sidelined when we pointed to the omissions.

Some of these issues, of course, are faced by leaders of all genders and backgrounds, but based on our past experience as leaders before taking these positions and the fact that each of us was, in our respective spaces, the only person of color in the room, we were well aware of and sensitive to the feeling of invisibility engendered by the framework of whiteness that was deeply ingrained in our institutions and at the root of the differential treatment we observed in comparison to our white male and female colleagues. We realized that the playing field was not level at all and that in too many instances, we did not have access to the necessary information, tools, or professional regard as white colleagues at our same level. Because we were outside of the box, which they constructed and in which they placed us as token Black representatives, our unpredicted actions and successful undertakings were more often than not either treated with suspicion or not acknowledged at all. The resistance we faced caused a feeling of being under surveillance, especially when people charged us with being too angry or oversensitive when we were simply offering a viewpoint counter to the status quo or dared to point out racial inequities. These responses of resistance and reticence constituted a form of institutional gaslighting, suggesting that we had overstepped our boundaries and perhaps even insulted their efforts meant to instill diversity and inclusion and to remove any suggestion of institutional racism. In such instances, instead of being a partner to that struggle, persons of color become ungrateful guests, Ahmed points out, who have overstayed their welcome. She concludes, "People of color in white organizations are treated as guests, temporary residents ... on condition that they return that hospitality by integrating into a common organizational culture, or by 'being' diverse, and allowing institutions to celebrate their diversity" (43).

UNVEILING "THE LIE"

In her candid and astute analysis of the dilemma of Black women academics at PWIs, "Why I Clap Back Against Racist Trolls Who Attack Black Women Academics," Stacey Patton offers perspectives on how institutional whiteness threatens professional efficacy and ability and the ability of Black women academics to succeed. Her observations offer lessons not only for Black leaders but especially for those institutional leaders at PWIs who would claim to have established an unassailable commitment to and embodiment of diversity, thereby presumably removing the charge of institutional racism and the perception of whiteness. Additionally, her words are important for Black administrators who are trying to make sense of nonsense in an unforgiving racial hierarchy and call our attention to the betrayal experienced by people of color who are part of the higher education workforce. She correctly notes,

> Universities want to create the illusion of diversity and to profit from that illusion, but they are showing little interest in making campus classrooms and curricula more inclusive, more welcoming, more honest, more intellectually rigorous. Once Faculty of Color are inside the building, once Students of Color pay their tuition and have their picture taken for the university website, all bets are off. The message we receive is clear: We got you for what we need, now sit down, shut up, and be counted for our diversity report while we pat ourselves on the back and call it "progress." (338)

Pointing to the lack of honesty and betrayal in institutional intention to foster diversity and inclusion, Patton echoes Derrick Bell's warning about white domination in our society and exposes what Eddie Glaude, Jr., deftly posits as the lie "that allows, and has always allowed, America to avoid facing the truth about its unjust treatment of black people and how it deforms the soul of the country. The lie cuts deep into the American psyche. It secures our national innocence in the face of ugliness and evil we have done" (8–9). He shines a light on the "architecture" or set of lies that are the basis for the value gap that sees Black people as inferior while upholding "the idea that in America white lives have always mattered more than the lives of others" (7).

Thus, the lie that has preserved white domination and has been a basis for racial inequity in America is also the source of the enduring whiteness of higher education. It has had a differential impact on people of color at all levels and will continue to perpetuate these circumstances if the issue is not addressed at the highest levels of leadership. The neoliberal white stance of many individuals and institutions correctly insists that attention to diversity is essential, yet they seem to feel that this stated commitment of intent, replicated in countless diversity statements and plans promoting each institution's mission and image, somehow exempts them from the charge of racism. Yet the word *racism* is avoided at all costs or used sparingly to designate someone who has committed an overt act of discrimination or other racial debasements.

Individuals refuse to acknowledge their complicity in systemic racism in any number of everyday actions because it is contrary to their progressive views of equality and images of themselves, for, as Robin DiAngelo explains, their binary worldview of racists as mean or bad people and everyone else—presumably nonracists—prevents them from understanding or accepting the fact that people "don't have to intend to exclude for the results of our actions to be exclusion," as with, for instance, cases of implicit bias or microaggressions (xiv). Speaking about the aversion of whites to talking about race, DiAngelo names this phenomenon *white fragility* and argues that what sounds like an easily injured and vulnerable response becomes a "sociology of dominance" that silences people of color who are berated and reproached for calling attention to racial harm (113). Ahmed goes a step further by suggesting that individuals within educational institutions sometimes find it convenient to attribute responsibility for the problem of whiteness and systemic racism to the institutional structure; the institution, in turn, seeks to relieve itself of blame by "recognizing institutional racism.... The institution, 'having confessed' to racism might be understood as on the road to recovery ... [and] is getting over it" (47). As a result, neither the "fragile" individuals outside and within the institution will take on aggressive responsibility for addressing racism nor will the institution, which has apologized and considers its *mea culpa* an absolution of wrongdoing. Deciding it has substantially addressed the cause and effects of racial disparity going forward, the institution thus abrogates responsibility, thereby leaving the framework of institutional whiteness intact.

The racial vantage point manipulated by whiteness and which perpetuates the lie stands in stark contrast to the perspective of Black people who are unwillingly entangled in an oppressive hierarchy generated by the lie. In his book, *Drylongso: A Self-Portrait of Black America*, anthropologist John Langston Gwaltney relied on the voices and observations of African Americans to demonstrate, as one of his participants stated, "drylongso, the way people really are most of the time together enough to do what we have to do to be decent people" (xxii). Through their actual words and narratives, these willing contributors present themselves as who "we really are." In so doing, they offer insightful commentaries on the nature of race and racism. Most pointedly, their unvarnished assessments highlight the profound impact of white privilege and power on both the Black and white psyches. For us, enacting the leadership role of Black deans brought into stark relief the impact of the "lie" that imprisons both races, as well as the differences between us and our white colleagues. To be sure, we inhabited the same role as deans as our white counterparts but from dramatically different racial vantage points.

Jackson Jordon, one of Gwaltney's contributors, sees the major difference between the two races as a game in which white people (bluffers) "think they can hide the fact that they generally do not know what they are doing." Moreover, he continues, "We [Black people] don't tell them that we *know* that they are trying to convince themselves that they are what they would like to be" (99). Because of the pervasive nature of this lie, Black people cannot reveal what they know but instead must be careful about what they say. Black people must depend on themselves. And they must be ready to do three or four more things, depending on how they feel (99). That is why, Jordon concludes, "Black people love justice because it is denied them" (99–100). For us, then, the concept of "drylongso" stands for our commitment to be treated just like other human beings without the added layer of biased judgments and preconceived assessments. The notion of drylongso guided our actions, even when those actions met with the cynicism and skepticism of systemic racism. We knew, to paraphrase Alberta Roberts, another of Gwaltney's contributors, that the biggest difference between us and our white colleague deans was that we knew when we were playing (103). Roberts contends that white people want to play all the time and won't admit that they are playing. Specifically, they pretend that "what's out here is not really out here" (106). As Black deans, we could not play with the truth nor count on others to accept, without critique or exception, that our version of reality was indisputable and always trustworthy. Instead, too often, we found ourselves in the unenviable position of dismantling the "lie" of our inherent incompetence, even in the face of repeated examples of competence, internally through the initiatives we developed and led at our institutions and, externally, in the national recognition those same initiatives received. As one of our provosts once said, "You don't dean like any other dean on 'the Bluff'" and he did not mean it as a compliment. No, we definitely were not playing but, to our dismay, our colleague deans and the administrators to whom we reported chose to ignore the evidence and instead embraced the lie that rendered our accomplishments visibly invisible. And, even more galling, they easily dismissed those accomplishments as anomalies rather than compelling examples of our leadership acumen.

TRANSFORMING THE MARGINS
AS OUTSIDER-WITHIN

Having served as department heads at a PWI before becoming deans, we were confident in the knowledge and skills that we brought to our positions, which swept us into greater responsibilities and a new context as we now reported to our respective immediate superiors, the provosts. Throughout our careers, we had always dealt with and been able to prevail against challenges of institutional whiteness, but we learned that maintaining balance as one moved up the institutional ladder became more precarious and could threaten one's position. It was, in a sense, like climbing a mountain that became more slippery and perilous to navigate, given the shifts in atmosphere (e.g., change in strategic direction based on legislature or board mandates or the unforeseen departure of a president or provost) or the emergence of an overhanging cloud or impenetrable fog (e.g., lack of transparency and shared governance) that made it difficult to secure our footing.

Imbued within all of this, of course, is your position within a space of whiteness in which you are climbing the mountain without the guidance afforded others—that is, situated in the margins and isolated among others all seeking the heights. You are standing outside on the inside—that is, carrying the status of *outsider-within*, a term used by Patricia Hill Collins to describe the position of Black women in the workforce in general and Black women creating Black feminist scholarship (11, 16). The terminology aptly fits the stance of Black women in higher education leadership who also face an institutional system of governance that in a number of ways has become arcane and does not meet the needs of its workforce. These Black women, who "claim the space in between, who theorize and practice from the space in between, are often at odds with the academic establishment, where knowledge is defined in racist and patriarchal ways and grounded as either/ors, top-downs, and theory-practice splits" (Baszile 200).

Thus, there is the feeling of being further pushed to the margins, but for us, that space was instead our place of refuge and resistance in our determination to enact strategies that would enable us to prevail in the face of adversities. The margins became for us what bell hooks envisions as a space of openness that "nourishes the possibility of radical perspective from which to see and create, to imagine alternatives, new worlds" (150). That place of refuge in the margin enabled us to focus on fostering truth and a culture of integrity, whereby we were willing to compromise but not to *be* compromised. While higher education touts the importance of a culture of integrity and accountability as formative principles for an ethic that guides the educational mission (Levin 31), those principles often get lost in favor of a "culture of celebrity," (32) desiring to market a profile that will enhance revenue, improve academic ranking, and win positive regard from benefactors such as governing boards, businesses, and alumni.

For us, the impetus to follow and promote a culture of integrity and accountability was a sustaining force with roots in legacies of determination, resourcefulness, and unfathomable persistence that sustained our ancestors, who for generations fought from the margins through eras of the Middle Passage, slavery, antebellum life, and codified segregation of Jim Crow legislation up to more recent conflicts over assaults on civil rights and racial justice. One of the tropes we are fond of using to describe our experience of enacting our role as deans is that of the intricate eighteenth-century cakewalk or complicated dance routine that the enslaved performed. While the idea of executing an action in a manner that is seemingly a "cakewalk" or "piece of cake" has come to mean carrying out something in a manner that appears straightforward and handled with ease, the original meaning referred to an elaborate, intricate dance done in slave quarters on occasional parties held by plantation owners for the enslaved, who would dance to compete for a prized cake. It is thought that they mimicked the intricate steps to a European style of dance executed by plantation owners and possibly that the creative and more exaggerated version performed by them was intended to mock the dancing they had seen performed by the plantation owners (Gandhi).

However effortless and natural their dancing appeared, it called for reserve and power to execute while retaining equanimity in their precarious position. Their actions were not performed solely for winning an award or "taking the cake" but were indicative of their using a rare opportunity to demonstrate their unique resourcefulness, wit, and sense of worth. The cakewalk also represented a moment in time when daily assaults on their physical and emotional well-being were eclipsed by intricate and well-planned moves that mirrored and reaffirmed their self-efficacy and a form of racial liberation. They found a way to find moments of joy and achievement, not in meeting the demands of those who claimed to own them but, if only briefly, to free their minds of oppression and despair and occupy the margin imagined by hooks to be a creative space of resistance that sparks creativity. In this mindset, the lie is set aside and, bell hooks contends, "we are transformed [and] make radical creative space ... which gives us a new location from which to articulate our sense of the world" (153). In obtaining our positions as deans, the prize for us was not a tangible one nor one of recognition and popularity; it instead was the satisfaction of insistently enacting a culture of integrity to help others and to focus on social justice in ways that negated the lie and dismissed the value gap on which it is based. In our role as deans who were at times relegated to the margins, we encountered, as did Du Bois and countless others who followed, "a past that is not past" and confronted within the realm of institutional whiteness "the ongoing problem of Black exclusion from social, political, and cultural belonging" (Sharpe 13–14).

Of course, there is a personal cost in all this—anger, feelings of betrayal, sadness, and other psychic injuries caused by actions that are rooted in the fears and biases of others. Even when we thought we had made progress, some days it suddenly felt as if we were starting all over, but we persisted with knowledge we did not have before. While we were at times confounded and dismayed by what we observed, looking beyond that disappointment and focusing on intent would more often than not lead to a positive end. In such situations,

> anger about internal neglect is replaced by joy in the successes of students or collaborative opportunities to build with colleagues at other institutions; disappointment in reversal of promised funding or space receded and turned into reassurance in creative alternative resolutions generated by staff and colleagues seeking positive change or unexpected and, even in some cases, sudden victories. (Hodges and Welch 125)

Thus, we were able to persist because the struggles made us appreciate the triumphs even more, and to do otherwise would mean abdication. For example, we used external collaboration with leaders of color at other PWIs to strategize and receive and offer mentoring. We learned to identify and cultivate unexpected white allies within our institutions. We engaged vigorously in professional organizations that helped us develop ideas and, by our presence, brought visibility to our units and institutions.

WHAT DOES IT MEAN TO DISMANTLE INSTITUTIONAL WHITENESS?

The differential impact of COVID-19 on communities of color and the senseless murders of Black youths and adults at the hands of corrupt police officers are stark reminders that schools and higher education institutions must play a role in redressing these social impairments within their organizations as a model for the broader social panorama. If higher education is to survive and retain its relevance, past history must be stood on end and toppled to be replaced by new operational tools and a new direction that fit the changing demographics of our country in order to achieve sustained transformation.

Reading from her poem "On the Pulse of Morning" at the inauguration of William Jefferson Clinton, Maya Angelou reminded us that while we cannot undo painful historical events, we must face them with courage so that we do not relive mistakes of the past. With this idea in the back of our minds, we asked ourselves many times what we could do in our roles as deans and continue to do in connections outside of that role to help disassemble a structure grounded in whiteness and wholly inadequate not only to serve the current higher education workforce but also unprepared to meet the needs of the rapidly increasing demographic shift in which people of color will be in the majority. Up to this point, changes in the structure in higher education key leadership roles have been all too slow and lag far behind the demographic changes. And too often, after leaders are convinced or forced to make changes meant to redress inequities, the original intent of those changes too quickly evaporates when a minimal and artificial indication of compliance (generally by numbers) is met. The institution, with the curious agility of a salamander, grows a new limb, or lie, that might be in a new form but replicates the previous disparities.

Given our experiences, what leadership strategies might we suggest, not as panaceas but as serious points of departure for others to consider as they navigate ever-changing administrative landscapes? First, it is important for women of color and white allies to unapologetically tell our stories. Stories contain the authenticity to challenge and "disrupt the culture of power" (Baszile 200). Thus, as Black women, grounded in the tradition of Harriet Tubman (Moses), Sojourner Truth, Lorraine Hansberry, and Maya Angelou, we must revisit the painful legacies of racism, willingly "walking over the broken glass" of these experiences to advance to a more just future.

Yet, in committing to "witness," we wrote our truth without tears because, "in the end, we retained the integrity with which we entered the
leadership role.... We each set out to fulfill our charge as deans and, in
doing so, learned a great deal about cultural politics and expectations of
leadership, about important principles for developing leaders in complex
social settings, and about ourselves" (Hodges and Welch 126). We hold
ourselves responsible for passing on that legacy of determination and
recording our truth in the face of the lie to which we have been tethered
and from which we must break free. However, we are *not* responsible for
helping white folks, even our most ardent allies, understand our pain or
empathize without the need to act, nor do we want to shed tears that enable white dilettantes to "playact" with us in healing conversations about
race that allow for staged recriminations built on our pain, whitewash-
ing our strategies, while tinkering around the edges of systemic racism.
In short, we will *not* allow our stories to be used to perpetuate the lie.

Instead, we intend for our counter-stories to provide a record of pain,
labor, and triumph that, we hope, serve as a resource for those who follow in our footsteps. And while we tell these truths without tears, it
is not without personal costs. There were times when we experienced
emotional and physical ills, which we took home to mend, after which
we returned to our roles refreshed by the victory of enacting those roles
with honesty and integrity. Rather than shedding tears, we chose to respond to racism with righteous anger. For, as Audre Lorde points out,
"Women responding to racism means women responding to anger, the
anger of exclusion, of unquestioned privilege, of racial distortions, of silence, of ill-use, stereotyping, defensiveness, misnaming, betrayal, and
co-optation" (124). Lorde insists that anger channeled into a creative understanding of our differences becomes productive, allowing us to "transform difference through insight into power. For anger between peers
births change, not destruction, and the discomfort and sense of loss it
causes is not fatal, but a sign of growth" (131). A second strategy we offer involves promoting firmly and adamantly a vision for leadership that

challenges the status quo while bringing added value to the institution's mission. This is a shared strategy, one that demands both individual and institutional commitment.

What then must be the charge to our white colleagues in leadership positions? In higher education, as with all organizations, commitment to racial equity must be initiated at the top and advanced by those in key leadership positions. They must engage with leaders of color and skillful diversity practitioners in honest conversations and welcome these partners to participate in framing a new structure and way of operating. The lie must be destroyed, but to do so leaders must own the lie; that is, they must acknowledge it and their participation in sustaining it to hasten its destruction. Everyone will not have the same beliefs and attitudes, but each must start where they are, and all must commit to moving forward. That involves taking a hard look at and generating discussions on several aspects of an institution's operations. This is not easy work for individual leaders to undertake, but it must be pursued, particularly when the initiatives they develop can serve as models of, and even the motivation for, substantive change. In advancing this strategy, we suggest three key points to consider.

First, it is essential to change the narrative on leadership in higher education—that is, to break away from the imagined model of the visionary leader whose famous (and in some cases notorious) past record, it is believed, holds the answer to heightening the institution's visibility, standing, and appeal. The institution not only must take a hard look at how leaders are selected by listening to and hearing disparate voices from all parts of the campus and community but also must be proactive in engaging the new leader in genuine collaborative work on strategic planning.

Second, we must encourage leaders to alter internal structures within the institution that support impractical policies and outdated practices that obstruct change and serve only to support the status quo. Top-down paternalism and power hoarding stifle efforts to break down hierarchies that sustain racial and gender inequities. For example, at high research universities, long-standing models for rewarding success in responsibilities in teaching, research, and service fail to recognize in too many cases and at too many levels (chairs of disciplines, department heads, college deans, and provosts) how the three responsibilities closely overlap, or how, despite the university's desire to be recognized for community engagement, the importance of the intertwined roles of research and service and community engagement highlight the university's mission. Instead, administrators often devalue teaching and service in favor of scholarly research or creative achievement. As a result, people of color considering moving into administration often not only are in the minority but also have little power to alter the process for evaluation and therefore either remain fixed at their level, unable to move up, or they leave.

Finally, it is essential to revisit and deconstruct the language of diversity and inclusion in light of how the institution professes to promote equity and social justice. In other words, we must "keep asking what we are doing with diversity" (Ahmed 17). We must pose new questions and solutions for initiatives meant to address inequities fostered by institutional whiteness. In an essay suggesting that the language of diversity and inclusion is a tactic of appeasement and has become "ideologically neutral" by ignoring concepts of equity and justice needed to transform institutions, Davina-Lazarus Stewart poses several questions contrasting diversity and inclusion with equity and justice. While one could make the case that Stewart's reproach describes what does sometimes happen with efforts to improve diversity, we would argue that the two pairs are not mutually exclusive and do, instead, complement and enhance one another. The questions that Stewart supplies demonstrate our point:

> Diversity asks, "Who's in the room?" Equity responds: "Who is trying to get in the room but can't? Whose presence in the room is under threat of erasure?"

Inclusion asks, "Has everyone's idea been heard?" Justice responds, "Whose ideas won't be taken as seriously because they aren't in the majority?"

In other words, all the questions posed here by diversity, inclusion, equity, and justice need to be asked again and again to obliterate the lie of white superiority and domination. Those questions form part of the work that must be done to forge institutional visions of leadership that value and incorporate a variety of faces, voices, and ideas that will carry out the formative principles that higher education in the United States has always claimed as its foundation.

In the final analysis, fostering "good, necessary trouble" in pursuit of equality and justice is a leadership enterprise worth undertaking, an enterprise powerfully underscored in a recent NPR *Story Corps* segment called "'We Are Her Work': Remembering Grandma's Legacy." In having made sacrifices to support three generations and having been a strong voice in her community, Lola (Cresciana Tan), a Philippine native who immigrated to California, modeled for those around her the idea that "your *job* is something you leave at the end of the day. Your *work* is what you leave behind *after* you are gone" (Selby). As deans, we made noise and, we hope, enough good, necessary trouble to leave behind a difference.

WORKS CITED

Ahmed, Sara. *On Being Included: Racism and Diversity in Institutional Life.* Duke UP, 2012.

Angelou, Maya. *On the Pulse of Morning.* Random House, 1993.

Baszile, Denise Taliaferro. "In This Place Where I Don't Quite Belong: Claiming the Ontoepistemological In-Between." *From Oppression to Grace: Women of Color and Their Dilemmas Within the Academy*, edited by Theodorea Regina Berry and Nathalie D. Mizelle, Stylus, 2009, pp. 195–208.

Bell, Derrick. *And We Are Not Saved: The Elusive Quest for Racial Justice.* Basic Books, 1987.

Collins, Patricia Hill. *Black Feminist Thought: Knowledge, Consciousness, and the Politics of Empowerment.* Routledge, 1991.

DiAngelo, Robin. *White Fragility: Why It's So Hard for White People to Talk About Racism.* Beacon Press, 2018.

Du Bois, W.E.B. *The Souls of Black Folk: Essays and Sketches.* 1903. Dodd, Mead, 1979.

Espinosa, Lorelle L., et al. "Population Trends and Educational Attainment." *Race and Ethnicity in Higher Education: A Status Report*, edited by Lorelle L. Espinosa et al., *American Council on Education*, 2019, pp. 1–12, https://1xfsu 31b52d33idlp13twtos-wpengine.netdna-ssl.com/wp-content/uploads/2019 /02/REHE-Chapter-1-SA.pdf.

Gandhi, Lakshmi. "The Extraordinary Story of Why a 'Cakewalk' Wasn't Always Easy." *National Public Radio*, Dec. 2013, https://www.npr.org/sections /codeswitch/2013/12/23/256566647/the-extraordinary-story-of-why-a -cakewalk-wasnt-always-easy.

Glaude, Jr., Eddie S. *Begin Again: James Baldwin's America and Its Urgent Lessons for Our Own.* Crown, 2020.

Gwaltney, John Langston. *Drylongso: A Self-Portrait of Black America.* New Press, 1993.

Hodges, Carolyn R., and Olga M. Welch. *Truth Without Tears: African American Women Deans Share Lessons in Leadership.* Harvard Education Press, 2018.

hooks, bell. *Yearning: Race, Gender, and Cultural Politics.* South End Press, 1990.

Levin, Yuval. *A Time to Build: From Family and Community to Congress and the Campus, How Recommitting to Our Institutions Can Revive the American Dream.* Basic Books, 2020.

Lewis, John [@repjohnlewis]. "Make some noise and get in good trouble, necessary trouble." Twitter, 27 June 2018, https://twitter.com/repjohnlewis/status /1011991303599607808?cxt=HHwWgMC27dKuqIscAAAA.

Lorde, Audre. *Sister Outsider: Essays and Speeches.* Crossing Press, 1984.

Patton, Stacey. "Why I Clap Back Against Racist Trolls Who Attack Black Women Academics." *Presumed Incompetent II*, edited by Yolanda Flores Niemann et al., UP of Colorado, 2020, pp. 332–40.

Selby, Abe. "'We Are Her Work': Remembering Grandma's Legacy." *National Public Radio*, 2020, https://www.npr.org/2020/11/27/938589603/we-are-her -work-remembering-grandmas-legacy.

Seltzer, Rick. "Failing to Keep Up." *Inside Higher Ed*, Mar. 2017, https://www .insidehighered.com/news/2017/03/02/racial-gap-among-senior-admin istrators-widens.

Sharpe, Christina. *In the Wake: On Blackness and Being*. Duke UP, 2016.

Stewart, DaFina-Lazarus. "Language of Appeasement." *Inside Higher Ed*, Mar. 2017, https://www.insidehighered.com/views/2017/03/30/colleges-need -language-shift-not-one-you-think-essay.

Whitford, Emma. "There Are So Few That Have Made Their Way." *Inside Higher Ed*, Oct. 2020, https://www.insidehighered.com/news/2020/10/28 /black-administrators-are-too-rare-top-ranks-higher-education-it%E2%80 %99s-not-just-pipeline.

3

ALIGNING NARRATIVES, ALIGNING PRIORITIES

Untangling the Emotional and Administrative Labor of Advising in Liberal Arts Colleges

JENNIFER SANTOS ESPERANZA

A dvisement has become one of the distinctive features of small liberal arts colleges (SLACs) in the United States. In addition to ensuring that students complete their academic requirements for graduation, the advising relationship between faculty members and students is promoted as a high-impact practice that can lead to better outcomes in student persistence, retention, and overall satisfaction (Drake; Kuh; Kuh and Hu; Tinto, "Stages of Departure," *Leaving College*, "Student Retention"). Unlike larger colleges/universities with units dedicated exclusively to advisement, SLAC faculty members do the bulk of this work, which necessitates more contact hours between faculty advisors with their students. SLAC faculty mentors work to usher students through their academic requirements, monitor their intellectual growth and career preparedness, and occasionally counsel students through their psychosocial adjustment to college life. These responsibilities mean that faculty who serve in this capacity are evaluated not only for their performance in teaching, scholarly activities, and committee service to the campus but also for their contributions to advisement.

Female faculty, and particularly those of color, find themselves especially vulnerable under these conditions. While there are formal, administrative standards by which their labor is evaluated while on the tenure clock, female faculty of color are often called upon to take up additional forms of invisible labor, especially in advising. For at least two decades now, higher education research has documented these inequities and revealed high levels of job dissatisfaction, stress, anxiety, and burnout among female faculty of color (Gutiérrez y Muhs et al.; Lambie and Williamson; Osajima). This is largely due to the slow pace (if not outright resistance) of higher education to institute the type of deep culture change that reflects the needs of its increasingly diverse professoriate (Ahmed).

In this chapter, I share some of my own experiences as a woman of color in pursuit of developing a leadership trajectory within higher education. In my case, I briefly held the role of faculty director of advisement at my SLAC. During my pre-tenure years, I learned and implemented a set of advising strategies that were designed for assisting marginalized students but could be adapted for all types of students. A few years after receiving tenure, I was appointed to become the faculty director of my institution's first-year and transfer advising program, in which my goal was to create a culture change in undergraduate advising: one that deliberately took a decolonized approach. My goal was to dismantle the culture of whiteness traditionally found within college advising: a type of mentoring style that favored norms of white, middle-class, and cisgender student behaviors. Instead, my plan was to promote advising practices that centered the needs of our most marginalized students, to critically question assumptions about what makes a "good student," and to use culturally relevant practices of academic interventions. I had also planned to install more formal mechanisms for advisor training and evaluation such that mentoring students did not fall largely on the shoulders of female faculty and faculty of color. Yet as I will discuss in this chapter, these plans were derailed in ways that echo recurring forms of institutionalized racism and whiteness that have yet to be fully expunged from higher education.

I am the first Asian American female to gain tenure at Beloit College, a SLAC located in southern Wisconsin. I share my story not as *the* case of a female faculty member of color but as *a* case, among many, that demonstrates the continued reinforcement of gendered, racial, and cultural stereotypes at predominantly white institutions (PWIs). I hope to address a few of the broader questions presented in this edited volume, particularly what it means to embody change as a leader of color in spaces historically created around normative masculinity and whiteness, especially as it pertains to ideas of what makes a "good" leader. This involves a frank discussion about the forms of structural violence experienced by female faculty of color; violence that is often myopically perpetrated by administrators at PWIs.

MENTORING IN ACADEMIA: UNEVEN AND UNNATURAL TERRAIN

Advising at SLACs is generally a two-dimensional undertaking, which Margaret Freije aptly characterizes as a dual practice of monitoring and mentoring. Monitoring entails helping students navigate the curriculum: walking students through all college requirements that reflect the breadth of a liberal arts education, helping students select courses for their major, and making sure requirements are completed in a timely manner. As these are responsibilities that rely largely on logistical planning and a concrete set of guidelines designed around the institution's graduation requirements, faculty success in this area can easily be measured by retention and graduation rates.

The second, more ambiguous dimension of advising involves mentoring. While the term is defined differently and liberally across higher education, most definitions recognize the importance of a role model who provides students with emotional and psychological support, along with academic and career advice. If successful, this type of support can contribute to a student's persistence through graduation (Jacobi). But the ambiguity around mentorship arises from the types of emotional labor that faculty are rarely trained to teach, nor can it easily be measured with quantitative data.

In short, SLACs acknowledge the benefit of advisor-mentors for student success and retention, but it is still a nebulous field that has yet to clearly define its methods, success indicators, and modes for faculty development (Crisp and Cruz). As college student demographics across the United States increasingly become more diverse, there is an even greater need for faculty advisors to mentor students on issues of persistence and belonging. This is especially the case at PWIs, where students from underrepresented minority groups likely make up a small percentage of the student body and often struggle with adjustment to the institution. In this chapter, I call attention to the reality that female faculty, and specifically female faculty of color, have been relegated to do this work of mentorship. I argue that this inequity is informed by misguided racial and gender stereotypes and threatens to stall the type of real institutional culture change that is long overdue.

THE INEQUITIES OF EMOTIONAL LABOR

As a faculty member at a small liberal arts college, I experienced the inequity of advisement from the very beginning. Soon after my arrival, my colleagues would often direct international, students of color, first-generation, and low-income students to meet with me during office hours if these students needed support regarding adjustment, identity, and other psychosocial issues. Two other female faculty of color and I were hired that year, and the buzz around campus seemed to be that there were *finally* professors of color with whom students could talk and relate. I was viewed as having a sympathetic ear for issues of cultural adjustment, familial expectations, and other dilemmas that international, first-generation, low-income, and minority students grapple with during their college years. Couched in terms of being an especially "approachable" faculty member, my colleagues had (deliberately or inadvertently) naturalized my ability to counsel students in such matters.

However, I had not been at the institution long enough for my new colleagues to know me personally, nor for them to be familiar with my capacity for mentoring. I can only surmise that my presumed approachability had been informed by racial and gender stereotypes of Asian Americans. Often viewed as a "model minority," Asian Americans are framed as polite, law-abiding (nonconfrontational) individuals who demonstrate and encourage high academic achievement (Blackburn). My collegiality, my short stature, and the fact that I am a Filipina American who comfortably code-switches between formal and informal registers, I believe, also factored into perceptions of my approachability. And the stereotypes were not just limited to students: faculty and staff colleagues also seemed at ease asking for advice on "awkward" matters. For example, at the end of my first year on the tenure clock, an administrator consulted with me as they wanted to ensure that the surnames of Asian students were correctly pronounced during the graduation ceremony. I was asked how to correctly pronounce the Chinese and Vietnamese surnames of our graduating students, although I have no cultural or linguistic affiliation with these ethnic groups. The administrator did not seem to think I would take offense to such a request.

I reluctantly and naively acquiesced to such demands of my time and labor, largely because this was my first year in a tenure-track position after having served as an adjunct instructor at two institutions over the course of four years. I was not going to risk the displeasure of my colleagues and superiors, especially as I had just secured my job at the height of a major economic recession. With student debt, a new house, and a second child on the way, I had numerous personal responsibilities to attend to, all the while juggling the demands of the tenure track. But the demand for my emotional labor made me aware of a few ironies that come specifically with being a female faculty of color on the tenure track.

The first irony is that while advising has become a major selling point for liberal arts college student recruitment, faculty members receive very little (if any) formal preparation for this aspect of their job. Informed by racial and gender stereotypes, advising is often approached as a "natural" skill that has, unfortunately, fallen on the shoulders of female faculty. With the exception of advising workshops and retreats, which still mostly focused on monitoring a student's academic progress, my new faculty peers and I were given little training on the mentoring side of advisement. As such, the burden remained heavier for female faculty of color to mentor students from various underrepresented demographics. We had become essentialized as persons willing and capable of doing the emotional labor of mentorship rather than seen as vulnerable new employees who were reluctant to protest when placed at the front lines of student retention.

The result of such an approach is that it reinforces a dangerous stereotype that mentoring is a natural talent that certain individuals possess rather than a professional skill to be developed. It also reinforces the myth that good mentorship can only happen between individuals of similar (real or perceived) social identities. In their five-year study on student experiences at liberal arts colleges, Cuba et al. write that first-year SLAC students often found their faculty advisors helpful only if the advising was limited to academic topics, and faculty seemed less comfortable taking on a deeper advising role (or what they characterize as the *in loco parentis* role; 115–16). Yet decades of higher education research show that advisement plays a crucial role in college student retention (Carstensen and Silerhorn; Habley; Light; Metzner; Pascarella and Terenzini; Seidman; Tinto, "Student Retention") and may even be "the single most underestimated characteristic of a successful college experience" (Light 8). So, what are the implications for female faculty, and especially female faculty of color, who take up the mentorship aspect of advising that their white, male counterparts have historically avoided?

This also enforces the second irony of faculty advisement at SLACs: female faculty of color are more vulnerable because mentorship is still measured by ambiguous standards. Faculty from historically underrepresented groups experience different realities and rules on the tenure track compared to their white, male, heterosexual colleagues (Niemann 448): What, exactly, counts as "good advisement?" In what ways has college advising been configured around expectations informed by a narrow set of cultural, gendered, racial, and class ideals that predate the demographics of today's professoriate?

For faculty on the tenure track, "teaching and advising" are often paired together as a singular area of review for a faculty member's tenure and promotion case. In my case, teaching was the only part of this dyad that was systematically evaluated and measured on an annual basis. At the second- and fourth-year reviews, the tenure and promotion committee evaluates advisement based on candidates' personal assessment and summarization of their advising. Aside from these personal narratives, my own advising record was not formally assessed until the year I went up for tenure. During that time, any students I may have *taught* in the past were contacted by email and asked to fill out an online survey to rate my advising style and invited to add additional commentary if they chose to. This left out numerous students whom I had mentored over the years, who were not enrolled in any courses I taught. This was largely the case for international and domestic minority students in the science, technology, engineering, and mathematics fields whom I advised, yet they had never (or rarely) taken my courses. The timing of such a survey also missed opportunities for current students to comment on my strengths and areas of improvement in order to gauge whether my mentoring strategies needed refining. Furthermore, the submission rate of completed surveys was too low to draw any significant conclusions about my advising record.

Surveys do not always obtain a full picture of the success of the advisor-student mentoring relationship, and in fact, faculty mentors and their students do not necessarily have similar expectations of the mentor-mentee relationship (Holt and Berwise). Neglecting to provide a clear definition or set of guideposts to monitor over a sustained period of time only reinforces perceptions of mentoring as a "natural," rather than developed, skill set.

REDEFINING AND DECOLONIZING ADVISING

During my pre-tenure years, I mentored students in a variety of ways: helping their adjustment to college-level academics, assisting in their search for summer jobs or internships, and listening to international students grapple with the culture shock of American college life are just a few examples of typical mentoring conversations. I did not always have an answer to their questions, but I also understood that mentoring can entail giving students the individual time and opportunity to talk about their academic and personal journeys. I quickly applied my ethnographic training in this capacity: asking open-ended questions as a means of getting consultants (in this case, students) to share their experiences, goals, and challenges. By listening and following up with the right questions, I found that students would inadvertently come up with their own solutions or at least gain a better perspective on adversity. Questions such as, "Tell me what high school was like for you," "What's your biggest struggle at the moment?," "What is a hobby or pastime that easily makes you lose track of time?," or "What do you wish people knew about you?" were particularly productive conversation starters, and often assisted in building rapport between myself and the students. Once students gained a level of trust with me, this led to more productive conversations around their personal, academic, and professional goals.

As the years progressed, I became more deliberate about taking part in development opportunities on campus that—while mostly designed around pedagogy—also proved to be instrumental for adopting an advising strategy that attended to the needs of historically underrepresented students. Several grant-funded opportunities on my campus provided the space where I could learn more. One initiative that I participated in (the Critical Engagement of Social Identities Project) was directed at increasing students' awareness of their political, social, and cultural locations as a means of understanding how such locations inform how they operate in the world. This grant allowed for a small number of faculty to meet on a weekly basis and prompted faculty participants to integrate storytelling, personal reflection, and academic autobiographies (how we came into our areas of study and expertise) into our pedagogies. A few years later, Beloit received another grant—this time to support the Decolonizing Pedagogies Project (DPP). The aim of the DPP was to assist faculty in identifying and unlearning the ways that their disciplines, methodologies, and pedagogies had been influenced by colonialist epistemologies. For a few years, I had also served as a faculty moderator for a campus-wide conflict-resolution program, Sustained Dialogues. These activities, along with my own burgeoning side interest in live storytelling, became my training ground for cultivating a rich and culturally responsive practice for student advising and mentorship. My next step was to integrate some of these lessons into the classroom.

FROM CULTURALLY RELEVANT MENTORING
TO CULTURALLY RELEVANT PEDAGOGY

As with many colleges and universities across the United States, first-year students at Beloit College take a seminar in addition to their regular course load. The first-year seminar is usually taught by a faculty member who serves as the students' initial academic advisor until they have officially declared their majors. The faculty member chooses the topic of their seminar and teaches it in a way that introduces students to college-level reading, writing, and critical analysis, all while fostering a sense of community within the small class cohort (usually between twelve to eighteen students). Such seminars are a standard feature of the first-year college experience (Pascarella and Terenzini; Porter and Swing), and Beloit College was among the first cohort of institutions in the United States to adopt this approach. At Beloit, all pre-tenured faculty lead a First-Year Initiative (FYI) seminar at least once before going up for tenure review, as it is assumed to be the primary avenue where they will learn the mechanics of liberal arts–style advisement. In the spring and summer months before leading the FYI seminar, participating instructors attend a series of advising workshops run by the faculty coordinator of first and transfer student advising. The workshops are varied and cover topics such as assignment design, advising international students, and teaching writing skills.

My FYI seminars were on the topic of taste and aesthetics. My own research interests involve the political economy of consumerism, and I designed a freshman seminar that would prompt students to engage in the type of exploration that would normalize the process of personal reflection and critical self-inquiry. The course encouraged students to develop a self-narrative in various mediums (writing, public speaking, digital storytelling, and podcasts). Informed by the fruitful mentoring conversations I'd had with students during my office hours, I wanted students to understand that their identities are ". . . not cognitive structures but are carefully constructed in discourse" (Schiffrin and De Fina 3). In the first-year seminar, students were asked to tell the story of their lives, through a critical analysis of their likes and dislikes over their lifetimes thus far. These exercises in critical self-reflection were also punctuated by readings and discussions about changes in trends and tastes for food, music, and art. By learning about changes in taste, and by regularly reflecting upon their own likes and dislikes, my FYI seminars became spaces for students to normalize the idea that personal and intellectual development is not fixed, but subject to change and external influences.

The goal was to design a seminar that prompted students to explore who they are, their likes and dislikes, and what they are learning about themselves by being in a new setting—college. This is a form of decolonized pedagogy: using personal narratives and integrating sensory and aesthetic experiences as a legitimate tool of intellectual exploration. And by starting at a relatively easy topic—one's personal taste in food, art, music, and movies—the idea was to ensure that students from a wide variety of backgrounds (but especially students from low-income, historically marginalized backgrounds), would arrive to class without feeling that they lacked the cultural capital to succeed in their first year of college. Their life experiences, frames of reference, and identities were valid starting points for college-level inquiry and discussion.

Also referred to as culturally relevant pedagogy, this style of "pedagogy [provides] a way for students to maintain their cultural integrity while succeeding academically" (Ladson-Billings 476). Students were assigned to write critical reviews of their favorite movies or to write a narrative of their favorite food after reading Marcel Proust's famous ode to the Madeleine cookie from *Remembrance of Things Past*. I was impressed by the intellectual and personal growth that I observed among students from my FYI seminars and even more so by seeing them thrive until their final year.

When the opportunity became open for a new faculty director to lead Beloit College's advising program, I expressed an interest to the provost about taking on this role. By this stage in my career, I had successfully gained tenure and was looking to cultivate a leadership profile by starting with something I found fulfilling: advising and mentoring. After many years of having my colleagues send students my way for a variety of advisement issues, and in witnessing the successes of teaching a culturally relevant seminar course for first-year students, it made sense that I pursue a leadership position in an area where I felt both confident and competent.

As faculty director of the first-year and transfer advising program, I could share some of the best practices I had developed over the years. By sharing successful advising and communication strategies with my colleagues, I hoped to begin circumventing the unequal mentoring load carried by female faculty of color. Essentially, I saw this as an opportunity to train faculty advisors more deliberately and more democratically. Advisor training would include teaching colleagues how to engage in deeper mentoring conversations with their students. Faculty advisors would also be encouraged to share their own academic and personal journeys with their students to normalize the struggles of college.

Upon receiving tenure and promotion, I received approval from the provost's office to become the next faculty director of Beloit College's advising program (then called the Initiatives Program). My preparations entailed job shadowing the outgoing faculty director during her final year to ensure a smooth transition of leadership. We met on a regular basis, and she was instrumental in sharing all of her resources with me: from deadlines and time lines for running the program throughout the academic year, explaining operational costs and spreadsheets from previous years, to pointing out the higher education literature on first-year experiences and student retention. She was a true mentor and my greatest advocate: she championed my advising record and underscored the importance of having our advising program spearheaded by a faculty woman of color. I also familiarized myself with the University of South Carolina's National Resource Center for the First-Year Experience and Students in Transition so that I could begin networking with researchers and fellow practitioners on undergraduate advising and mentoring programs.

A TRAJECTORY DERAILED

After a year of preparations, I finally served as the faculty director for my campus's Initiatives Program—overseeing first-year, second-year, and transfer student advising. During that time, I worked alongside the associate dean of students, who oversees the residential and student life side of programming. Unfortunately, in the middle of my first year as faculty director, a number of major institutional changes disrupted my plans. As with many SLACs, which had not been meeting their enrollment and fundraising goals over the years, my college made major budget cuts and changes in order to remain viable. The provost left the college, and an interim group of faculty took over leadership of academic affairs while a nationwide search for a new provost was underway. The college's operating budget, including programmatic funding for the Initiatives Program, was significantly reduced, as was our staff and faculty size (through early retirements and faculty/staff departures). The program I was now running could no longer offer stipends for participating faculty, and I now had to recruit faculty advisors from a smaller instructor pool. The most significant change, however, was that the college could no longer offer first-year interdisciplinary seminars as it had been doing for over thirty years. Short-staffed departments would lose much needed courses for their majors if the old seminar model continued subtracting one faculty-taught course from its curriculum every fall semester.

The opportunity to finally take a leadership role at my institution proved to be difficult under such circumstances, but I was willing to demonstrate that I was up for the challenge. I responded to this crisis by recruiting enough colleagues to teach introductory/first-year courses within their departments, in lieu of the freshman seminar. In addition to regular introductory course content (e.g., introduction to chemistry, beginning Russian, introduction to sociology, first-year writing seminars), these faculty instructors were asked to integrate advising and mentoring exercises, cohort-building activities, self-reflection writing assignments, and other research-proven practices that could still foster a high-impact, first-year experience. I had renamed this newly configured model the Spark Program—aimed to spark first-year students' interests in academic topics, community engagement, and self-exploration.

The arrival of a new provost during the following academic year proved to usher even more drastic changes across campus. I had not fully implemented and measured the success of the new Spark Program when the new provost came with a mandate to implement an even newer, more revised first-year advisement, orientation, and registration process. Over the course of a few months, I soon found myself lost in the shuffle of a reconfigured and reorganized advising program. My responsibilities soon shifted from director of student advisement to serving as the faculty director of summer orientation programs. At the request of the provost, I was tasked to redesign a summer orientation weekend for incoming students, centered around welcoming them and their parents to the campus community and getting students registered for their first semester courses. I immediately (and naively) accepted this position, not quite understanding that I had essentially been phased out of the leadership role that I had spent years preparing for.

A different faculty member was tapped to take the role of faculty director of advising—a white, female, junior colleague who had not yet received tenure. Under the new provost, a flurry of new task forces, working groups, and implementation teams dominated the campus agenda. My role had taken on a different iteration: from an administrative role leading the advising program to, instead, a role that appeared to be the equivalent of an events planner. I asked the provost to explain to me why my role had shifted so suddenly and abruptly, but I was only told that my new role was just as important and crucial to student retention. I was reassured that this new position was a good fit, as I had a reputation for being a "particularly good" community builder for students. This was not a satisfactory answer, as it failed to acknowledge the years of research and job shadowing I had invested in to become a good advisor and administrator. In addition, being recognized for my aptitude for community building was yet another backhanded compliment that hemmed me into doing more social and emotional labor and shut me out from taking on a leadership role.

I spent several months sitting in meetings for the college's new advising and orientation programs, though I could see, quite clearly, my role had become peripheral, and my presence was largely pro forma. My ideas for a robust orientation program were superficially acknowledged, and it was not long until a representative from student affairs communicated that I need not trouble myself with more orientation program planning meetings. The committee that I had been meeting with was now being led by an administrator from student affairs; they reassured me that "we've got it from here." I became dissatisfied with the disrespectful and demeaning situation I found myself in and promptly informed the provost that I would remove myself completely from any role involved with student advising, registration, and orientation programs.

ALIGNING MY NARRATIVE/ COUNTERSTORYTELLING

In their introductory chapter of *Presumed Incompetent*, Harris and Gonzalez write that "not only the demographics but the culture of academia is distinctly white, heterosexual, and middle- and upper-middle-class. Those who differ from this norm find themselves, to a greater or lesser degree, 'presumed incompetent' by students, colleagues, and administrators" (3). Since distancing myself from the advising program at my institution, I have revisited the events that led to, and ultimately derailed, my goal of assuming a leadership role at my institution. I have tried to make sense of how I had gone from a faculty director position, to orientation program coordinator, to being informed that my services were no longer necessary in the course of less than a year. I frequently fluctuated between feelings of self-doubt over my capabilities as an effective administrator, to self-blame over whether I could have done something so wrong as to warrant my removal from directing an important academic program.

And yet, my years of training around decolonized pedagogies have taught me the value of storytelling to make sense of "what had happened" and more specifically, counterstorytelling to make sense of what happened to me—a woman of color in a predominantly white space. Counterstorytelling is a technique used in critical race theory that reclaims the narratives of historically marginalized groups (Delgado and Stefancic). In doing so, they expose the workings of white privilege and institutional racism.

What does a counterstory of my experience with institutional whiteness look like? It is a narrative that realigns itself to expose the struggles of women of color in higher education. Counterstorytelling necessitates that I not bother wasting my time searching for reasons why I was removed from an administrative role. My counterstory is one that is aligned with exposing institutional whiteness at work: a woman of color was seen for years as a "naturally" gifted faculty advisor and community builder, but when there was an opportunity for her to handle advising and community building as an institutional leader, her colleagues and administrators did not trust her enough to take on that role, based on their biased, ethnocentric definitions of leadership. My counternarrative exposes the failure of my PWI to take the responsibility for recruiting and maintaining minority faculty to build fulfilling careers within the institution. My counternarrative highlights the shortcomings of my SLAC to champion faculty of color who seek to implement innovative and decolonized forms of advising to truly transform higher education.

While this chapter is a written counternarrative that shares what I have experienced, I choose to keep relatively silent when asked by my colleagues to discuss what happened. My silence is deliberate. As Margaret Montoya reminds us, women of color may use silence in a variety of ways (859). Our choice to remain silent at particular moments is not necessarily negative; many cultures use silence as a political stance, as a tool of resistance (852). I have experienced too many years of having to "prove" the structural violence I've experienced as a woman of color in academia. The culture of higher education, and particularly of PWIs, often puts an undue burden on people of color to provide "proof" of their experience with structural racism, and I am not interested in doing that again. And even when presenting narratives, evidence, or proof of such transgressions, we are still largely at a disadvantage—it is our word against the institutions'. Therefore, I have chosen to move forward and to pursue professional opportunities where I can practice advising and mentoring on my own terms and through other platforms. In her online article on institutional betrayal, Susan Shaw writes, "We are asked to represent diversity, but we are not given meaningful seats at the tables of power . . . but, even when we do, the institution betrays us." Inspired by these words, I have decided to control my narrative, realign my priorities, and no longer participate in my own oppression.

CREATING REAL CULTURE CHANGE: NEXT STEPS

The goal of this chapter was to share some of the obstacles that faculty women of color may face as they attempt to develop a leadership trajectory within PWIs. In my specific case, I wanted to lead the charge in changing student advising at SLACs, especially given the fact that the United States' college-bound students are becoming increasingly diverse. I would like to offer a few observations of where real institutional culture change can happen, especially in regard to advising programs and leadership roles for female faculty of color.

It is important to start off by debunking the myth that advising is a natural talent and one that female faculty of color "seem" to be particularly good at. Mentoring students through their academic and personal growth is a skill that is developed over time and differs from one individual advisor to another. To truly make institutional change, colleges and universities must critically reflect upon the ways they have put an undue burden on women of color to do this work. In addition, institutions (like SLACs) in which faculty members have considerable advising loads should adopt a formal process for measuring the efficacy of student advisement. Administrators and faculty should work together to identify the instruments and criteria through which faculty can be fairly evaluated.

Finally, institutions should be cognizant of their multiple biases when it comes to identifying who can occupy leadership roles. To what extent are notions about organizational skills, personality, collegiality, and other leadership qualities embedded in cultures of whiteness? This is especially true in moments when institutions undergo changes in leadership, mandate, and culture: look to see whether there are women of color at the table who hold integral roles in strategizing and implantation. If not, ask yourselves, why not?

WORKS CITED

Ahmed, Sara. *On Being Included: Racism and Diversity in Institutional Life*. Duke UP, 2012.

Blackburn, Sarah Soonling. "What Is the Model Minority Myth?" *Learning for Justice*, 2019, https://www.tolerance.org/magazine/what-is-the-model -minority-myth.

Carstensen, D. J., and C. Silberhorn. *A National Survey of Academic Advising (Final Report)*. American College Testing, 1979.

Crisp, G., and I. Cruz. "Mentoring College Students: A Critical Review of the Literature Between 1990 and 2007." *Research in Higher Education*, vol. 50, 2009, pp. 525–45.

Cuba, Lee, et al. *Practice for Life: Making Decisions in College*. Harvard UP, 2016.

Delgado, Richard, et al. *Critical Race Theory: An Introduction*. 2nd ed, New York UP, 2001.

Drake, J. K. "The Role of Academic Advising in Student Retention and Persistence." *About Campus*, vol. 16, no. 3, 2011, pp. 8–12.

Freije, Margaret. "Advising and the Liberal Arts: It Takes a College." *Peer Review: A Journal of the AACU*, vol. 10, no. 1, winter 2008, https://www.aacu.org /publications-research/periodicals/advising-and-liberal-arts-it-takes-college.

Gutiérrez y Muhs, Gabriella, et al., editors. *Presumed Incompetent: The Intersections of Race and Class for Women in Academia*. UP of Colorado, 2014.

Habley, W. R. "Academic Advising as a Field of Inquiry." *NACADA Journal*, vol. 29, no. 2, 2009, pp. 76–83.

Harris, Angela P., and Carmen G. Gonzalez. Introduction. *Presumed Incompetent*, edited by Gabriella Gutiérrez y Muhs et al., UP of Colorado, 2014, pp. 1–3.

Holt, Laura J., and Clifton A. Berwise. "Illuminating the Process of Peer Mon-
itoring: An Examination and Comparison of Peer Mentors' and First-Year
Students' Experiences." *Journal of The First-Year Experience & Students in
Transition*, vol. 24, no. 1, 2012, pp. 19–43.

Jacobi, M. "Mentoring and Undergraduate Academic Success: A Literature
Review." *Review of Educational Research*, vol. 61, no. 4, 1991, pp. 505–32.

Kuh, G. D. "What We're Learning About Student Engagement from NSSE."
Change, vol. 35, no. 2, 2003, pp. 24–32.

Kuh, G. D., and S. Hu. "The Effects of Student-Faculty Interaction in the 1990s."
Review of Higher Education, vol. 24, 2001, pp. 309–32.

Ladson-Billings, Gloria. "Culturally Relevant Pedagogy 2.0: a.k.a. the Remix."
Harvard Educational Review, vol. 84, 2014, pp. 74–84, https://doi.org/10.17763
/haer.84.1.p2rj131485484751.

Lambie, G. W., and L. L. Williamson. "The Challenge to Change from Guidance Counseling to School Counseling: A Historical Proposition." *Professional School Counseling*, vol. 8, 2004, pp. 124–31.

Light, Richard J. *Making the Most of College: Students Speak Their Minds*. Harvard
UP, 2001.

Metzner, Barbara S. "Perceived Quality of Academic Advising: The Effect on
Freshman Attrition." *American Educational Research Journal*, vol. 26, 1989, pp.
422–42, https://doi.org/10.3102/00028312026003422.

Montoya, Margaret E. "Silence and Silencing: Their Centripetal and Centrifu-
gal Forces in Cultural Expression, Pedagogy and Legal Discourse." *Michigan
Journal of Law Reform*, vol. 33, 2000, pp. 263–327.

Niemann, Yolanda Flores. "Lessons from the Experiences of Women of Color
Working in Academia." *Presumed Incompetent*, edited by Gabriella Gutié-
rez y Muhs et al., UP of Colorado, 2014, pp. 446–99.

Osajima, Keith. "Telling Our Stories to One Another." *Academe*, vol. 95, no. 3,
2009, pp. 28–29.

Pascarella, Ernest T., and Patrick T. Terenzini. *How College Affects Students: A
Third Decade of Research*. Jossey-Bass, 2005.

Porter, S. R., and R. L. Swing. "Understanding How First-Year Seminars Affect
Persistence." *Research in Higher Education*, vol. 47, 2006, pp. 89–109.

Proust, Marcel, et al. *Remembrance of Things Past*. Random House, 1934.

Schiffrin, Deborah, and Anna De Fina. Introduction. *Telling Stories: Language, Narrative, and Social Life*, edited by Deborah Schiffrin et al., Georgetown UP, 2010.

Seidman, A. *College Student Retention: Formula for Student Success*. Praeger, 2005.

Shaw, Susan. "No Longer Participating in Our Own Oppression." *Diverse Issues in Higher Education*, 13 Aug. 2020, https://diverseeducation.com/article/187527/.

Tinto, Vincent. *Leaving College: Rethinking the Causes and Cures of Student Attrition*. 2nd ed., U of Chicago P, 1993.

— — —. "Stages of Student Departure: Reflections on the Longitudinal Character of Student Leaving." *The Journal of Higher Education*, vol. 59, 1988, pp. 438–55.

— — —. *Student Retention and Graduation: Facing the Truth, Living with the Consequences*. The Pell Institute for the Study of Opportunity in Higher Education, 2004, http://files.eric.ed.gov/fulltext/ED519709.pdf.

4

ON THE PERILS AND OPPORTUNITIES OF INSTITUTIONALIZING DIVERSITY

A Collaborative Perspective from Academic Unit-Based Diversity Officers

M. CRISTINA ALCALDE AND CARMEN HENNE-OCHOA

nstitutions of higher education have long functioned as microcosms of society and its exclusionary practices (Chun and Evans; Stewart and Valian). To be sure, the COVID-19 pandemic and the civil unrest catalyzed by the murder of George Floyd only exacerbated long-standing challenges and laid bare the pervasive whiteness of academe and the dominance of normative identities in university administration. As our country has sought to reckon with its racist past and present, higher education has significantly accelerated its own efforts to address diversity, equity, and inclusion (DEI). Pushed to make diversity an explicit institutional goal, predominately white institutions (PWIs), for instance, have rushed to add institutional change agents, or chief diversity officers (CDO), to their senior leadership ranks (Williams and Wade-Golden; Worthington et al.). Seventy-two percent of CDO positions in 2012 had been created in the previous five years (Williams and Wade-Golden). A more recent analysis that surveyed 60 CDOs from major US research universities and liberal arts colleges noted that forty-three percent had been appointed in the last two years. Among those sixty CDOs, fifty-seven percent (34) are women (Pihakis et al.). This latter statistic warrants underscoring in that women, at every level of academic life, including senior diversity leadership positions, have made significant representational gains (Ballakrishnen et al.).

Yet, despite the increased presence and celebration of women in leadership positions, their work continues to be embedded within institutional environments that are putatively white and masculine. This reality is especially pronounced for women of color diversity leaders, whose unique leadership skills and contributions tend to be eclipsed by their having to work doubly hard to reach the levels of respect, autonomy, and power extended to traditional white male leadership across various realms (Matthew). Moreover, women of color diversity leaders confront a paradoxical mandate: they are formally charged with disrupting or "causing trouble" to existing structures at the same time as they are expected to prove and center loyalty to the structures and processes upon which the institution has been built. And, as other women of color scholars have rightly noted, "the higher the position, the more compliance is expected" of those who are most visible (Niemann 315). Like a good many other women of color diversity officers, we both have ample lived experience in our professional careers confronting the aforementioned double-edged directive.

In this chapter, we focus on the challenges we have encountered as unit-based diversity officers to identify opportunities and examine spaces of nuance and tension in the practice and embodiment of diversity work, which we affirm as inherently troublesome. Drawing on our personal experiences as administrators, our career trajectories, and existing scholarship, we bring a critical lens to bear on our experiences for what these reveal about the practice and embodiment of diversity work, and the connections between micro/interpersonal experiences and wider cultural and social meanings and understandings (Chang). Moreover, the lens we offer as unit-based academic diversity officers—the newest addition to the growing field of DEI in higher education—is a corrective to extant scholarship, which has tended to focus on the role and experiences of CDOs. While one of us (Cristina) currently holds a CDO role, the experiences we draw on for this chapter speak specifically to experiences as unit-based diversity leaders. Like CDOs, as unit-based diversity officers, we work toward advancing DEI, though the units in which we are housed significantly inform our roles. Some of us are full-time DEI staff administrators, while some of us are part-time faculty who return to our full-time teaching/research positions at the end of our administrative term. Enjoying varying degrees of autonomy, we are tasked with a range of responsibilities, including strategic planning and implementation, managing unit DEI budgets, and/or determining unit-wide DEI efforts.

As members of unit-level leadership teams at public Research 1 universities, we engage unit-level and university-wide challenges and opportunities. In the context of decentralized structures in which much of the diversity work in universities takes place, our analysis offers a nuanced and in-depth understanding of the structural and personal challenges and opportunities at the unit level as these intersect with broader patterns and structures. Cristina is an anthropologist who when we began writing this chapter served as professor of gender and women's studies and associate dean of inclusion and internationalization in a College of Arts and Sciences of approximately 470 faculty and 175 staff. She was one of two Latina full professors in the college, and the only person of color on the dean's leadership team. Since then, Cristina's institutional affiliation and position have changed; for this chapter, however, she draws on her experiences as a unit-based diversity officer at an R1 institution. Carmen is a sociologist by training and currently serves as assistant dean for diversity and inclusion in a liberal arts unit at an R1 institution. Her unit consists of approximately 1,400 faculty and 600 staff.

Until recently, she was the only woman of color on the senior leadership staff team. We both identify as Latinx and (im)migrant women of color. For both of us, our professional and personal commitments, as well as our outsider status—in part gleaned from our persistently low levels of representation among faculty and administrators in the academy—directly inform the diversity work we lead.

The experiences we present here portray our efforts advocating for change at the unit level all the while negotiating our own identities as Latinx women. While not exhaustive of the experiences faced by women of color diversity officers, we highlight the disproportionate amount of emotional and affective labor that is expended on behalf of and for the benefit of our academic institutions. We point to issues of (in)visibility/hypervisibility as central to understanding our experiences. And, as the last example presented by Cristina captures, challenging the status quo—in this case, disrupting patterns of whiteness via curricular reform—entails obstacles and contradictions that intersect at the university and unit levels. We intentionally examine both the centrality and the web of power structures that inform unit-level efforts, and the more nuanced and intimate ways in which our own embodied positionalities interact with those power structures.

Our chapter thus brings together the systemic and the personal and does so by amplifying the work of those who have centered trouble and risk as inherent to the embodiment and practice of diversity work (i.e., Ahmed, "Embodying Diversity," *Living a Feminist Life*, and *On Being*; and Chun and Feagin; Niemann et al.; Stewart and Valian; Whitaker and Grollman). As women of color diversity workers, it is not simply that we are perceived to cause trouble when we do diversity work, but that we *are* trouble by virtue of gendering and racializing the diversity work we lead. Our brown bodies are trouble in the sense that we are some*bodies* from outside, and, as transgressive Latinas, we are not infrequently perceived to be a threat and a liability to well-established institutional norms.

We acknowledge that "without senior leadership that focuses on driving the wheel of change . . . campuses will continue to flounder in their diversity efforts" (Williams, "Seven Recommendations" 53). That said, as diversity workers have experienced firsthand, the institutionalization of diversity leadership positions does not necessarily mean that the institution is willing to be transformed (Ahmed, *Living a Feminist Life*). And the diversity work we do as we attempt to transform our institutions is precisely the work that marks us as not quite inhabiting, or willing to inhabit, the norms of the institution (Ahmed, *Living a Feminist Life*)—norms that are largely founded on white hegemony (Chun and Feagin). We, therefore, find ourselves in the peculiar predicament of simultaneously working "for" and "against" our institutions, with our embodied identities adding a layer to how we navigate our work, as well as how it is perceived. For instance, our own disposition toward and adeptness (or lack thereof) at striking a balance in working for and against our institutions can, in any given context, elicit either approbation or disapprobation. The examples that follow illustrate how we each negotiate the politics of disrupting without being "too" disruptive, even as we and the boundaries within which we work are tacitly surveilled by those around us. As too many women of color diversity workers know firsthand, approbation or disapprobation of our performance doing diversity work can open or close doors (e.g., to meetings, opportunities, promotions). On the less dire—though not inconsequential—side, approval or objection can earn us certain labels: "aggressive," "demanding," "confrontational," "fiery." Certainly, the aforementioned labels are not epiphenomenal to one's identity but are rather intimately intertwined with our gendered and racialized embodiment. Our familiarity with this requires little explanation, and this reminder will suffice: the label "aggressive," for example, is reserved for women, particularly, for effective women in leadership positions who are perceived to be encroaching upon or making attacks on white, masculine work environments.

PUSHING AHEAD BEHIND THE CURTAIN: EMOTIONAL LABOR, INTENTIONALITY, AND DISRUPTION

A recent study on the experiences of academic unit diversity officers at the University of Michigan underscores that diversity officers unanimously agree that "interpersonal skills in order to build relationships and trust with diverse stakeholders" are central to being successful in the role (Grim, et al. 145). Our own experiences, and those of others with whom we are familiar, encourage us to more specifically name these interpersonal skills and their consequences as invisible affective labor and to underscore the intersecting roles of gender and race in these experiences and roles. As diversity officers, we strive to change cultures, becoming "institutional change agents" (Worthington and Smith) in spaces that both demand and persistently resist our work toward change.

Professionalization in preparation for faculty and leadership roles in academia rarely includes attention to emotional labor as a critical skill or expectation. However, for those of us who embody diversity personally and through our work in the realm of DEI, the reality is that emotional labor is an unwritten job expectation. The racialized and gendered weight of emotional labor, which includes both serving and caring for the emotional needs of others while managing and suppressing one's own emotional responses (Hochschild), is particularly poignant for women of color. We begin by providing some background on Cristina's role and experiences and then move on to share two brief examples from our experiences of diversity efforts and how they encompass emotional labor, intentionality, and both opportunities and costs associated with disruption.

Embodying diversity and accessibility at the college leadership level can demand a significant amount of emotional and affective labor of the individual in the service of the institution. In Cristina's case, she was the first associate dean in the college to have "inclusion" in her title

and focus specifically on diversity as part of her role. Almost immediately after she accepted the position, her calendar became stacked
with one-hour meetings with individual faculty. Some of these meetings
were in her office. For others, faculty requested to meet off campus so
they could feel more at ease. Some were scheduled, others unannounced
drop-ins. Cristina moved from one important and emotionally draining
meeting to the next, actively and empathetically listening, providing support, and taking notes about experiences shared with her. Faculty, most
of them women, and many of them women of color, shared with her
painful experiences of problematic interactions with their colleagues,
of being on the receiving end of coded gendered and racialized language, and of other daily microaggressions that resulted in both personal and professional harm. What she often heard is very much in line
with Fujiwara's own experience that in spite of the negative effects of actions and comments on her, for her colleagues "if actions do not appear
overt, like racial epithets or threats, then they do not constitute a serious problem" (107). The information she gathered from these meetings,
while likely not surprising to women of color in academia, was critical
in determining what policies and initiatives were most needed in the
college, so she could work to create and implement them. She regularly
left in a rush, after teaching and a series of meetings on college, university, and individual issues, making it barely on time to pick up her son
before after-school care closed.

While Cristina's calendar was initially filled with individual meetings,
her goal from the beginning was to create sustainable structural change.
Her approach was to examine smaller (and therefore more manageable)
distinct but interrelated issues, processes, and stated priorities and challenges systemically within the contexts in which they occurred at the departmental, unit, and university levels and more broadly across higher ed
contexts and to implement these at the college level. When the size and
structures of the broader university feel too large to change, her focus on

the college level became a way to begin to tackle some issues through a more contained, localized approach. Her focus on systemic structural change and her evidence-based perspective, however, was only possible through sustained engagement with the microlevel—whether through individual meetings or something else, where the day-to-day effects of structures are so intimately experienced. The affective labor of microlevel interactions of building trust, active listening, and management of emotional responses does not appear in evaluations or specific initiatives yet is foundational to identifying and bringing about needed forms of structural change and designing sustainable strategies. It serves the institution as well, as in the shape of contributions to community building and faculty retention.

In this context, it is also worth noting that while emotional openness is necessary in one realm for her role, in another realm, it must be securely guarded. As Cristina met with others in leadership positions, she was acutely aware that as the "diversity person" in the room, she was expected to push for change and that she inhabited the role of insider/outsider. Armed with her own experiences and those of colleagues, she was also aware that culture change takes time and that to actually be heard in those meetings, she must not only be intentional and strategic in how she presented topics and issues but also she must present them in ways that are not deemed too emotional, too angry, too subjective, or too extreme. That sort of self-awareness and self-management demand emotional labor in the service of persistently pushing for creating gradual, sustainable change for the institution to meet its stated goals of diversity and inclusion. Listening and being listened to are the bedrocks of change, and both demand unquantifiable amounts of invisible affective labor behind the curtains for those of us who are perceived as both trusted insiders and transgressive outsiders. These forms of affective labor often intersect with gendered and racialized power structures and hierarchies at the unit level, as the example Carmen shares in the next section underscores.

OLD HABITS DIE HARD:
MEN'S APPROPRIATION OF WOMEN'S WORK

In the academy, one of those institutional habits deeply entrenched within white masculine heteronormativity is men's appropriation of women's ideas and work. The terms *hepeaters*, *himitators*, and *bropropriators*—drawn from popular culture (see Bennett)—highlight just how commonplace and widespread this habit is within and outside academia. Much sociological and popular literature has analyzed men's appropriation of women's ideas and work in the context of gendered socialization and deeply ingrained individual and societal biases. We are taught, for instance, to associate authority and expertise with men and masculine traits—loudness, assertiveness, dauntlessness. Conversely, women's ideas, it is offered, are not clearly heard, and their work is not clearly seen because of our interactional and communication patterns. Women, we are reminded, are socialized to talk less, take less, share, interrupt less, and wait our turns. From a sociological perspective then, women are, therefore "predisposed" to take our cues from and listen to those (men) who speak and present loudly and with authority. This said, here we are less concerned with analyses that seek to explain—perhaps rationalize—why men appropriate women's ideas and work. Instead, drawing on her experience, Carmen shares the trouble caused in one instance where, as a diversity worker, she directly exposed and confronted an institutional habit. In particular, she focuses on the ways in which the degree of trouble caused and incurred is dependent on diversity workers' agility to strike a "good" or "acceptable" balance between working for and against the institution. In other words, on our agility to disrupt in a way that isn't too disruptive of the status quo.

The appropriation habit exists in institutional environments organized around the principles of hierarchy. Per the common understanding, a clear hierarchy is necessary to ensure a commanding form of leadership (Getha-Taylor). Among other things, hierarchy engenders loyalty (thereby aiding the institution's production and success), ensures a clear-cut chain of command considered important for an institution's operational smoothness (thereby mitigating chaos and confusion), and staves off competition and threats to the institution. For most, hierarchical organization is so natural in terms of ways of doing things and relating within the university that it is rarely, if ever, perceived, much less, questioned. For those who embody the norms of the institution, hierarchical ways of doing things and relating are habits that save time and trouble. It is within this context that one of Carmen's senior, white, male colleagues, henceforth Liam, asked her to do the work of conceptualizing her unit's first-ever diversity committee. She took on this task not only in her role as Liam's subordinate but also because Liam had never before this time occupied a diversity position. Thus, her taking on this task would save time and trouble.

For two weeks, she worked on this document that outlined the diversity committees' organizational and governance structure, its mission, and overall strategy for helping to integrate and institutionalize the unit's DEI priorities. When she completed it, Liam proposed that they present the diversity committee idea at the upcoming senior leadership meeting. At that time, Carmen was fairly new to her unit and was the only person of color on the senior staff leadership team. As a newcomer to the unit, she had heard the term "flattened" deployed in conversation to describe the tone of the senior leadership meetings. Its deployment, however, was more aspirational than true in practice. Still, she understood, and assumed, that she and Liam would copresent, this despite the fact that the final meeting agenda that was circulated had only his name next to "their" agenda item. More disconcerting, however, was that Carmen's name had been removed from the document that she had single-handedly produced and was distributed at the meeting. At that moment, she was struck by the thought of how much *more* trouble it had taken Liam to expunge her name than to leave it. Liam's name, however, did not appear in place of hers; indeed, it did not have to, precisely because hierarchical organization makes this redundant. That is, it is taken for granted that, on behalf of the institution, the occupier of a superior position has dominion over the work produced, whether or not such person contributed. Hierarchical organization, recall, is useful in that it serves to stave off competition, especially that which is threatening to white masculine heteronormative habits and ways of doing things.

Seeing that her name had been removed from the document to be presented, Carmen spent the first 45 minutes of the meeting *all up in her body*—agitated and perspiring, and anticipating how it'd go when it came time for them to present. When the time finally came, Liam presented her work for ten minutes. It was only toward the end that he asked if she had anything to add. Carmen chimed in, though she doesn't recall what she said. Even after Liam had finished presenting, she found it difficult to focus her attention on the remaining meeting business. Hence, she was relieved when the meeting came to an end, and she could return to her office to be alone. She was clearly shaken up, though this had nothing to do with a lack of familiarity with what she had just experienced. As earlier noted, women, and in particular, women of color, are all too familiar with having our knowledge and work appropriated and owned in ways that are both subtle and barefaced. In fact, the frequency of these experiences has meant that Carmen has developed the habit of including "Prepared by Carmen Henne-Ochoa, PhD" on any and all work for which she takes the lead or is the sole author. Rather, she was shaken by a certain feeling of defeat, of having had to sit through this again, silent and invisible. It was a difficult reminder to take in: what was for her a viscerally disorienting and discomforting experience (necessarily) remained an invisible experience for everybody else in the room. That is, since the disruption of hierarchical processes always has the potential to cause discomfort to those who inhabit the institution's white masculine norms and habits, diversity workers must work hard to mitigate or make invisible their own unease so as to ensure others' comfort.

Working for and to transform the institution, then, necessarily involves comfort work. And this specific instance of comfort work, like most other instances doing such work, warranted a measured approach. While much is said about the value of and openness to authenticity and transparency—speaking truth to power—when one follows through, those on the receiving end oftentimes have little appreciation for the truth. With this front of mind, Carmen did not engage in any dramatic moment of speaking truth to Liam at the leadership meeting. She did, however, later confront him. She devoted close to a week thinking and strategizing about how she would approach him about his appropriation of her work. She decided that she would address this at their upcoming one-on-one regularly scheduled meeting. Would she give Liam a heads-up so that he could anticipate the matter? How exactly would she bring it up during their meeting? What words would she use to describe "her" issue? There are diplomatic as well as disastrous ways of speaking the truth. Many of us have experienced an instance or two in the latter category and have subsequently suffered the implications. Hence, this time around, she needed to take care to minimize risk to herself, including not coming off as too "aggressive" or "accusatory." A diplomatic and collaborative approach, therefore, meant giving Liam the courtesy of time to anticipate her confrontation. She thus included Liam's appropriation of her work as an item on their upcoming meeting agenda. Following a conversation with a trusted colleague (herself a diversity worker), Carmen momentarily imagined including the agenda item as "stealing my work." Such imagining, however, was more a way to vent and give expression to her anger and frustration. Indeed, even the term "appropriation" could risk her coming off as too confrontational—she'd be accusing Liam of having taken possession of her work without permission or acknowledgment. In the end, she included the item on the agenda as "attribution"—a more delicate and charitable term with a less accusatory ring to it. Framing it as "attribution" was a way to play the game, a way to preserve the hierarchical structure and protect its occupiers. Framing it as "attribution" allows us to pretend that the troubling issue is more about what one can *give* than about what one has *taken*.

After a long unnerving wait, Carmen broached with Liam the matter of attribution, which she had strategically placed last on the agenda. She recounted her experience at the senior staff leadership meeting. However, she did so quickly, simply recounting her "surprise" at having seen her name removed from the document she produced. She conveyed that her "sensitivity" to questions of attribution stems from the frequency with which the work and ideas of women, and of women of color, in particular, are appropriated. Most of her energy, however, was spent on conveying to Liam how, going forward, she hoped they might both acknowledge their individual contributions toward the efforts and goals of the unit. Indeed, framing it in terms of benefits to the institution—an institution, moreover, that has said it wants to be transformed—is a way to be heard by those in power. "Walking her talk," she explained to Liam, was key to maintaining a level of integrity in her facilitation of sessions with faculty focused on standing up to sexism and gender injustice in the workplace. In that context, Carmen stressed that she'd continue to include her name on documents for which she was the sole author. Throughout, Liam listened. At no point, however, was there an explicit acknowledgment or an apology on his part.

At the microlevel, there was no interpersonal eruption caused by Carmen's confrontation. Also, as far as she is aware, this particular instance of her speaking truth to power did not carry grave professional trouble or risk for her, though the potential was certainly present. At worse, it took a couple of weeks before she and Liam were able to move beyond the awkwardness caused by the confrontation. Yet, it's important to acknowledge here that the level of professional risk incurred is often inversely related to the level of personal/embodied trouble experienced by diversity workers. This specific instance of diversity work that involved exposing an institutional habit consumed no less than two hundred minutes of Carmen's physical, mental, and emotional labor (she had subsequently codified the time for a presentation she delivered at a women's leadership conference). Indeed, the simultaneous work of transforming institutions and minimizing one's own professional trouble and risk requires an inordinate amount of strategy and energy. In Carmen's example, consider the time (three hours and twenty minutes) and associated energy this one particular instance involved: making invisible her viscerally disorienting experience at the meeting during which Liam owned her work, making sense of and recounting to family and trusted colleagues what she had experienced, strategizing and planning how to bring up the issue with her white, male, senior colleague, and prioritizing his comfort in a way that she could avoid incurring additional trouble and risk.

As the literature amply documents, and as the foregoing examples affirm, diversity work demands a disproportionate and considerable amount of emotional and affective labor from women of color diversity workers. To reiterate, however, such labor remains largely invisible, not because no one sees it (administrators, faculty, and students are well aware of and reap its benefits) but because institutions do not value it with the currency they typically use to reward other professional work. Without such labor, it would be difficult—indeed, impossible—for institutions to accomplish the "culture-shifting" type of work they have tasked the diversity workers with doing. As our examples moreover capture, additionally troublesome for women of color diversity workers is that the emotional and affective labor we expend as we intentionally work to make visible those things that the institution does "not" see—and often expends its own energy on not seeing—can and does render us invisible or hypervisible. As Cristina and Carmen expand upon next, working within a paradox of invisibility/hypervisibility is a familiar experience for women of color diversity workers. Together, their examples speak to the ways in which, as Settles et al. remind us, visibility, hypervisibility, and invisibility coexist and point directly to power relations.

PUSHING FOR VISIBILITY AND ACTION:
LATINX IDENTITIES IN A PWI

Visibility is often the first step to acknowledgment and inclusion in broader discussions of diversity. During a student panel on Latinx experiences Cristina organized and moderated, one student panelist lamented the low numbers of Latinx faculty and the few courses offered on Latinx histories. Another student expressed dissatisfaction with the lack of understanding about Latinx identities in the university. These students' experiences are far from rare. While nationally Latinx students make up nineteen percent of undergraduates, universities continue to lag behind in the recruitment and retention of Latinx faculty (Cantú), with many universities struggling to maintain three percent Latinx faculty. Latinx students, faculty, and staff continue to not see themselves reflected in faculty ranks and in senior leadership positions, even as for some university administrators these forms of exclusion continue to be invisible.

In the context of National Hispanic Heritage Month and to complement unit-level programming such as the student panel referred to earlier, in Cristina's role as faculty chair of the university's Latinx Affinity Group, she approached the university's central diversity office to ask about planned events and statements. Affinity groups are university-wide, identity-based groups, and the group had typically met twice a semester. A request she had previously made to the central diversity office, under which the affinity groups are housed, to support workshops on Latinx mentorship and leadership experiences, as well as on anti-Blackness among Latinxs during this pandemic year, had been denied, with the explanation that there simply was not any funding available. At the same time as the request was denied, a new centralized DEI planning group (in which no senior Latinx members were included as part of the leadership of the group) was announced and proudly discussed in various public news releases. As Hispanic Heritage Month was well underway and there was no action from any central offices, Cristina asked about planned activities and statements. The answer came quickly: no events had been planned, but would she like to write a short statement that the university public relations office might share more broadly about the contributions of Latinx to the university and how the university valued Latinx community members?

Cristina declined to write a statement for the university, noting that her unit-level focus precluded her from speaking on behalf of the university's efforts across all colleges to support Latinx faculty, staff, and students. Instead, working with the university-wide Latinx faculty and staff group, she and the group then submitted an invitation to members of senior leadership to join the group for a dialogue to discuss concerns and experiences of Latinx community members. The group viewed the dialogue as a way to educate university leaders, increase visibility, and push for commitment to begin work toward needed changes. Before the meeting would be agreed to, however, a senior leader asked Cristina to individually meet with that person to provide more background and an explanation of the topics of discussion for the dialogue the letter of invitation listed.

In the context of Latinx stereotypes as too loud, transgressive, deficient in academic preparation, and lacking language skills, seeking visibility as a first step in disrupting systems of exclusion must be persistent yet presented in ways that those in power can recognize. During two meetings and one phone call, Cristina provided background information on various areas, measuring her words and assuring the senior leader that the group wished to engage in a *dialogue* while drawing on her expertise on DEI work, Latinx identities and experiences, and higher education. Rather than feeling her expertise was being valued, however, she experienced these preparatory meetings as tests to see if the group would indeed "behave" during the type of meeting being requested, and to determine how unwieldy or not the group and demands might be, based on her own performance and self-presentation. In granting a meeting, the

Latinx identities and areas of discussion being presented would become visible, and once granted the meeting and seen, there was the danger for upper administration that what was seen could not be unseen. The meeting was granted, with the caveat that it be limited to a very small group of representatives—that, then, necessitated the work of preparing for the meeting with the group of representatives.

In the previous example, Cristina embodied not simply diversity but more specifically the sort of diversity (Latinx) that the university had paid little attention to even as Latinx student numbers increased. Once almost invisible, her speaking up suddenly made her too visible, and the response was both tokenizing and perpetuated a pattern of asking individuals who embody diversity to contribute their often unpaid and invisible labor for the sake of institutional public image management (in the case of a celebratory statement) to maintain a positive institutional image. On the one hand, symbolic attention during a specially marked month, such as Hispanic Heritage Month, does little to change underlying structural issues that have long sustained exclusions and invisibility. On the other hand, as symptoms of a much larger problem of exclusionary practices and structures, it is institutional indifference and associated absences that become quite visible to those of us looking. Ensuring the first meeting with senior leaders to address broader structural issues necessitated that through Cristina's embodiment of diversity and as representative of a large and diverse group she demonstrate her willingness to push, but not too far, and to speak truth to power, but not too loudly. Cristina's self-presentation and choice of words carried both the potential to help disrupt these structures and bring in more voices through securing a first meeting and the risk of closing that possibility through missteps.

Working at the unit level allows us to both call out the institution for persistent exclusions and to work on changing those structures and practices from a more localized level that allows us to engage with broader structures and collaborate across units. The work of disrupting exclusionary practices can take the form of our individual embodiment and our claims to specific forms of diversity, our refusal to be complicit in institutional public image management in ways that reinforce invisibility of everyday exclusionary practices, the push to be included on diversity committees and initiatives at the university level, and the development of inclusive local unit-level policies, practices, and programming that can then be expanded. As we disrupt, we continue to take on the invisible labor of advocating for, mentoring, making visible, and supporting students, faculty, and staff—those whose identities have yet to be adequately recognized and included in university-wide action-focused plans.

THE PARADOX OF (IN)VISIBILITY/HYPERVISIBILITY: DOING DIVERSITY WORK WITHIN THE "FAMILY"

As diversity officers, we enjoy some level of visibility—and thus legitimacy and authority—given the leadership positions we occupy. However, like other faculty of color in the academy, in certain contexts, our marginalized group status can render us invisible in terms of our personal identities. For some of us, we are denied a place and a voice at the table. For others, our education and preparedness may be questioned, and our achievements undervalued, overlooked, and even ignored. Still, in a different context, who we are (or who we are taken to be) is magnified and scrutinized. Our numerical minority or "token" status, our race and gender markers that differentiate us from dominant group members, and, in particular, our deviance from and challenge of dominant norms can make us hypervisible (Settles et al.).

The following example speaks to ways in which, in our practice and embodiment of diversity work, we traverse and negotiate (in)visibility/hypervisibility. Here, Carmen focuses on an affinity space, what we often call a "home" away from home. For many of us, affinity spaces are where we go to find meaningful community and refuge and also where many of us go to momentarily escape our hypervisible (token) status and the white gaze we otherwise encounter throughout our academic settings. Affinity spaces are where many of us speak openly, share experiences of marginalization and overcoming, raucously celebrate wins and accomplishments, and where we build networks and establish relationships. Many of us feel seen, heard, and valued in such spaces. By no means, however, have affinity spaces been an escape from the range of persistent challenges and inequities that women face in the academy, particularly as these relate to gender bias and the gendered expectations that constantly operate as contextual surround thereby shaping both institutional processes and interpersonal interactions.

Carmen is reminded of the ways in which a masculine presence, and a nagging sexist tone, structured the Latinx affinity space in question. The affinity group's planning board and (informal) welcoming committee included several male colleagues. It was not difficult to see why they were well positioned and identified for leadership roles within the group. They are professionally accomplished, thereby making good role models and potential mentors to other Latinx members. Individually and collectively, they are also outspoken, attentive, and gregarious—all of which made for consistently entertaining monthly sessions for the 30–60 faculty and staff usually in attendance. One Latino colleague, in particular, had a knack for lively entertaining. Not infrequently, however, this came at the expense of the tokenization of a much-loved and respected, albeit reserved, Latina colleague with a long tenure at the institution and a deep commitment to the Latinx community. His public introductions of, addresses to, and engagements with her were often awkward. In one salient and unequivocally problematic instance, while introducing her to new affinity group members, much like one might find at a momentous large Latinx family gathering honoring the matriarch, he deliberated at length about her maternal virtues: caring, nurturing, supportive, selfless, and loyal. With a generous display of deference to her (physically bowing down to her and frequently gesturing in her direction), his deliberation included memorable anecdotes of her service to and love for the Latinx community. However, nothing of what he said—not a single word—spoke to her decades-long professional experience or expertise. This introduction and commendation of our Latina colleague can certainly be described and may have even been experienced by those in attendance, as collegial, warm, and affectionate. Yet at that moment, and as our Latina colleague stood on the floor, composed and seemingly reactionless, one could not help but notice the reinstantiation, seamlessly transposed from the home to the work environment, of the idealized female figure. To be sure, our Latino colleague's performance was a convivial rendition and a potent reminder—whether real or romanticized—of women's place in the structural and sociocultural order of things. As Latina women, we are visible; indeed, we are best seen when we approximate the *mamita* archetype: amiable, maternal, nurturing, selfless, and strong, so long as such strength is nonthreatening and remains submissive to the male ordering of things.

At the meeting that day, no one, including Carmen, disrupted the sociocultural order. It was not that the performance was illegible, or the annoyance on the part of some, indiscernible. As a way to preserve the group's "familial" relationships, it was much easier to sit with the annoyance and, via silence, simply nod to the (supposed) matriarchal centrality of our collective experience. Others in the group, we might imagine, chose to see the sexist behavior on display through a more flexible and culturally congruent lens; for indeed, deference and condescension, one might put forth, can be (re)interpreted as respect and protection. Fast-forward several months following that meeting, a male colleague on the affinity group's planning board invited Carmen to present on the diversity work she does with faculty and staff. She accepted the invitation, doing so with the intention of making up for her earlier missed opportunity to speak up and feeling further galvanized by an egregious sexist experience with another Latino colleague in a senior leadership position. Sharing here extensive details of this egregious sexist experience makes Carmen further vulnerable. Suffice it to say that, as in her earlier example, this one too involved a case of appropriation. In this instance, however, the tensions and nuances were somewhat more delicate. First, following substantial deliberation, she chose to respond via email to her Latino colleague and included several others who were directly involved. Second, this had the feel and trappings of an interfamilial situation, where the clear sentiment—and expectation—is that it is best to leave the family's dirty laundry unaired, or otherwise do the airing within the family. Carmen did neither, which came with certain consequences (that here will be left unsaid). Her message to this Latino colleague contained the following words: "... those of us [who are Latinx or who work in the realm of DEI] are not immune from reproducing various forms of inequity and oppression. Often the labor (intellectual and physical) of women, and, in particular, women of color, goes unnoticed (worst yet, it gets appropriated)."

Coming back to the presentation Carmen was to give at the affinity group's lunch meeting, while initially hesitant, she made up her mind to speak on the traditional and cultural habits and practices that privilege men and subordinate women and that stand in the way of progress within the Latinx community. Those weren't precisely the terms she used to convey her proposed talk to her Latino colleague who had invited her, though she did make it clear that she'd be addressing, in a general way, gender (in)equity. He didn't have anything to say in response, though Carmen wasn't expecting much in the way of a positive reaction. Ahead of her presentation, she also made a point of informing her other Latino colleague (with whom she had had that egregious sexist experience) of her presentation topic. He regularly attended the lunch meetings, and she saw informing him as offering him the opportunity to save face. As far as she was aware, no one who would be present at the lunch meeting knew of their highly uncomfortable exchange. Still, in light of their exchange, she gathered he'd feel quite uneasy being present while she addressed issues of gender within and with the Latinx community. He didn't show up. His wife, however, whom Carmen had never before seen at any of the lunch meetings, was in attendance. In fact, she sat herself a couple of seats away from where Carmen was seated.

Overall, Carmen's presentation was well received, though there was a pronounced difference in terms of its reception by male and female colleagues. From their seats, female colleagues' body language consistently affirmed, at times spiritedly, the content of her presentation. In contrast, male colleagues' faces and their physical posturing showed a kind of distancing in some and curiosity in others. During the Q&A portion of her talk, all the questions posed came from female colleagues. Moreover, following her presentation, several colleagues approached her with additional questions, all of them women except one—a male graduate student who, after having thanked her, proceeded to share with her and other women standing nearby his own experiences with gender discrimination. As for Carmen's male colleague who invited her to give the presentation, he left the room without any acknowledgment. The personal note of thanks or the customary note of acknowledgment never arrived; she was rendered invisible. Hegemonic masculinity—whether in the culturally relevant form of machismo or otherwise—rarely responds kindly when an invitation to speak is repaid with an interrogation of its core ethos of subordinating women.

As we earlier noted, as diversity workers, we strive to change institutional cultures in spaces that both demand and persistently resist our work toward change. But, it's important to note that doing such work in familiar or "familial" spaces significantly compounds the stressors we experience and the risks we incur. For, indeed, we face what, in a different context, Hochschild calls *the second shift* (Hochschild and Machung). That is, after doing the work of resisting and challenging in a predominately white workspace, one that scrutinizes us and makes us hypervisible, we then (re)turn "home" only to undertake what feels like a disproportionate amount of "familial" responsibility in doing the work of transforming institutional culture. Perhaps most difficult of all is that our nonconformity to and intentional disruption of cultural scripts that uphold masculine and heteronormative practices and ideals, leaves us feeling invisible in these spaces of familial affinity. Indeed, we become isolated in those very spaces, often the only spaces, where we go to be heard and seen outside of the token status we inhabit within the wider university community.

In the example that follows, we further explore this token status and the affective labor often attached to it in exploring the behind-the-scenes efforts associated with macrolevel curricular changes to recognize and make racialized histories and experiences more visible.

OPPORTUNITIES FOR DISRUPTING WHITENESS: CURRICULUM AND A RACE AND ETHNICITY COURSE REQUIREMENT

In the context of widespread protests and activism and more attention to experiences behind Black Lives Matter on and off campus, universities have paid increasing attention to their existing curricula and how they do or do not prepare students to learn about and engage with the histories and realities of oppression, exclusion, and racism in the United States and the world more broadly. While a few universities have had race and ethnicity requirements for quite some time (for example, the University of Michigan's requirement dates back to 1990), many others are only beginning serious discussions about this. At the very least, such a requirement would help address the experience of Black, Indigenous, and People of Color students (including those in the Latinx student panel referred to earlier) who repeatedly make visible ways in which their peers, faculty, and institution do not seem to understand or value their histories and experiences. In Cristina's institution at the time we began writing this chapter, the lack of movement on this front at the university level resulted in concentrated efforts within her unit for a college-specific diversity requirement for undergraduate students. These efforts predate the COVID-19 pandemic and the anti-racist protests of the last two years, yet the issuing of university-, college-, and department-level anti-racist statements in response to anti-Asian and anti-Black violence and racism provided new visibility to these efforts. In fall 2020, nine months after college approval of the requirement and following multiple hurdles, the requirement passed the first university-wide approval process. It passed final Senate approval during Spring 2021, with a planned effective starting date of fall 2021. Examining some aspects of the process in more detail provides additional insights into the obstacles faced in attempts to embed diversity into institutional culture beginning with one unit as a way to disrupt patterns of whiteness.

The goal of the proposed college requirement was to draw on existing expertise across departments to educate regarding one central and persistent, complex set of phenomena—race, racism, racialization. Courses that met the requirement would address one or more criteria related to race and ethnicity through more than fifty percent of class time, course materials, and student assignments. The proposed course requirement would not add additional credit hours since the courses also fulfill other requirements, could be taken at any point before graduation, and would only be enforced starting with the fall 2021 cohort. We explicitly decided to name it "Race and Ethnicity" instead of, for example, the much broader "Diversity" to name and focus on these areas. Emphasizing and making visible specific areas within the catch-all term of *diversity* is an important first step in educating about diverse histories and experiences and contributing to cultural competence.

In Cristina's administrative role, she coordinated efforts to put together the proposal for the requirement, working with a faculty committee and other administrators. She facilitated discussions about the requirement in various college committees and discussions and was approached and given input about the proposed requirement by faculty. The three main areas of concern for those who expressed reservations about moving forward with the requirement were that the requirement (1) promoted a particular political ideology, (2) created a hierarchy of inequalities by focusing on race and ethnicity, and (3) emphasized the negative and oppressive over the positive aspects of race and ethnicity. Cristina drew on research and best practices across institutions as she made sure to manage her own reactions in listening to colleagues express some of these concerns.

While not expressed in such terms, concerns that a race and ethnicity requirement represented indoctrination rather than education derive from a broader trend of interpreting the term diversity as part of a leftist agenda to suppress conservative voices, oppress white males, and shut down free speech. This concern could be partly addressed by pointing to the variety of disciplines and faculty involved in advocating for the requirement across institutions and in the college. Course topics further provided ways to underscore the educational importance of focusing on historically marginalized voices to provide students with a more holistic view of society. More personally, the part of these discussions that Cristina grew to cherish most was responding that the requirement could easily include a course on the construction and practice of whiteness and inviting concerned faculty to assist in identifying such a course.

The concern that the requirement created a hierarchy of inequalities came from those who worried that other identities and more specifically that gender, socioeconomic class, and religion were being relegated to a lesser status. Emphasizing that this requirement complemented rather than competed with existing courses and providing examples of courses that took an intersectional approach to address race as well as gender and other identities while meeting the criteria for the requirement assuaged some concerns. As an immigrant and scholar in gender and women's studies, Cristina also drew on her own embodied experiences and courses she designed and taught as examples of how a focus on race and ethnicity does not preclude the inclusion of other markers of difference and in fact often necessitates the inclusion of other identity markers.

The third concern, that the requirement put too much focus on oppression, speaks to what we consider to be the celebratory politics attached to diversity work. One person suggested that we consider a more "positive" framing of the learning outcomes attached to the requirement.

As Ahmed has noted, the constant reality and danger are that for institutions "diversity becomes a technology of happiness: through diversity, the organisation is represented 'happily' as 'getting along', as committed to equality, as anti-racist" ("Embodying Diversity" 46). At the level of curriculum and individual courses, diversity may be expected to focus on celebrating cultural heritage at the expense of analyzing histories of discrimination, violence, and oppression. A focus on oppressive structures provides multiple ways to examine agency and activism—for example, in a social movements or activism course—without becoming an empty celebration of identity and difference.

Cristina's role in leading efforts to pass the course requirement inevitably also had an effect on which faculty felt comfortable directly approaching her with their concerns and how they did so. For example, the concern, or complaint, that the requirement was too negative (i.e., focus on inequalities and oppressive structures) and should have a more positive framing was not initially expressed to her directly. Instead, it came up during the college-level discussion for a final vote, after input had already been collected from all college-level committees and from individual departments. Two senior white male colleagues expressed concern about the focus on inequalities and therefore negative framing of the requirement. In some ways, we can compare these comments to uninvited comments Cristina received earlier in her career from students and peers about how she should "lighten up some" because of her attention to racism, racialization, exclusion, and violence. While colleagues may feel less comfortable expressing this directly to her at this point in her career, the desire to do so may still be there.

Later, during a meeting with a cross-college university committee, a white male faculty member in the college who had not expressed any reservations about the requirement during multiple discussions at the college level suddenly became the strongest opponent of the requirement at the university level, furiously looking for technicalities that would prevent the requirement from passing. At one point, he brought up the new Africana and African American studies major as an example of how this requirement would create an undue burden on some majors by forcing students to take the course requirement. The irony of using this particular major, whose faculty had been particularly vocal in supporting this requirement, to argue against the requirement was not lost on those advocating for the requirement. Having openly presented this requirement as the first step toward what Cristina and others hope would be a university-wide requirement, Cristina was prepared to continue to cause trouble as she and others pushed it forward. In doing diversity work and pushing for culture change, diversity workers must be prepared to see some who had been assumed to be silent allies suddenly finding their voice in opposition to a proposed change, the more real an initiative becomes.

FORGING AHEAD, BETWEEN THE SYSTEMIC AND UNIT LEVELS

Institutions of higher education approach diversity as an area of strategic importance, even as they continue to be characterized by their resistance to change (Williams, *Strategic Diversity Leadership*). Such resistance to change, as we have sought to show in this chapter, must also be understood and appreciated at the unit level, and as it is specifically negotiated by and impacts unit-based academic diversity officers. We do not negate the importance of scholarship that focuses on the role of CDOs and, by extension, on macro- or systemic-level processes within the institution. We do, however, stress that such focus must not come at the expense of devoting little attention to the unit level, where the more localized work that is necessary to initiate and sustain broader organizational change takes place, and to the microprocesses manifested at the unit level.

As Williams (*Strategic Diversity Leadership*) notes, it is mid-level leaders within academic units who are often tasked with a significant portion of change management labor that is critical to enhancing DEI.

Among those who may be characterized as mid-level diversity workers, graduate diversity officers, for instance, are essential in fostering inclusive environments and student success through their focused work on graduate student recruitment and retention efforts to increase graduate students of color. This work, to be sure, is neither carried out in a vacuum nor divorced from existing microlevel departmental structures, processes, and cultures (Griffin et al.) but, in fact, is a lens into understanding the ways in which broader organizational change happens. It is also the case that, especially at institutions where academic units (i.e., schools and colleges within an institution) have significant autonomy, academic deans and school- or college-level leadership can catalyze or otherwise inhibit organizational change for inclusion and equity through leadership roles, structures, and practices within their units.

In sharing and analyzing our experiences, we have drawn necessary attention to the ways in which diversity officers—generally women and people of color (Williams and Wade-Golden)—work against leadership roles and institutional practices and norms modeled after white, elite forms of masculinity (Liu). In the context of our commitment to diversity work, we highlighted our own affective labor, as well as our experience and negotiation of invisibility/hypervisibility as we seek to make visible those institutional processes that delegitimize our own and others' identities and contributions within higher education. We made this the focus here precisely because it is important to show that the costs of this type of affective personal and interpersonal work are rarely quantified, even as they consistently eat away at the physical and emotional well-being of those doing the work in the service not only of social change but also specifically of the institutions we inhabit. And, to be clear, it is those who have been historically marginalized in higher education who are now called upon to lead change from within the institution.

As we have shown throughout this chapter, the expectation on the part of the institution is that change and transformation must be (or are best) ushered in with just the right amount of diversity infusion. That is, in and through our institutional leadership roles, we must push enough to visibly display diversity but not enough to necessarily destabilize the foundations on which exclusive and inequitable processes and practices can continue to exist. The tensions, nuances, challenges, as well as opportunities—both at the personal and institutional levels—would be difficult to observe without looking closely at micro- and personal/interpersonal processes. Perhaps most importantly, at least from the perspective of the institution that is looking to be transformed and looking for evidence of its transformation, too quickly jumping to solely looking at systemic or macrolevel structures obscures the very ways in which it is through microprocesses that macroprocesses often produce their effects.

WORKS CITED

Ahmed, Sara. "Embodying Diversity: Problems and Paradoxes for Black Feminists." *Race, Ethnicity, and Education*, vol. 12, no. 1, 2009, pp. 41–52.

———. *On Being Included: Racism and Diversity in Institutional Life*. Duke UP, 2012.

———. *Living a Feminist Life*. Duke UP, 2017.

Ballakrishnen, Swethaa, et al. "Intentional Invisibility: Professional Women and the Navigation of Workplace Constraints." *Sociological Perspectives*, vol. 62, no. 1, 2019, pp. 23–41.

Bennett, Jessica. *Feminist Fight Club: A Survival Manual for a Sexist Workplace*. Penguin UK, 2016.

Cantú, Aaron. "Universities Try to Catch Up to Their Growing Latinx Populations." *The Hechinger Report*, 4 June 2019, https://hechingerreport.org/universities-try-to-catch-up-to-their-growing-latinx-populations/.

Chang, Heewon. *Autoethnography as Method*. Left Coast Press, 2008.

Chun, Edna, and Alvin Evans. *Leading a Diversity Culture Shift in Higher Education Comprehensive Organizational Learning Strategies*. Routledge, 2018.

Chun, Edna B., and Joe Feagin. *Rethinking Diversity Frameworks in Higher Education*. Routledge, 2019.

Fujiwara, Lynn. "Racial Harm in a Predominantly White 'Liberal' University: An Institutional Autoethnography of White Fragility." *Presumed Incompetent II: Race, Class, Power, and Resistance of Women in Academia*, edited by Yolanda Flores Niemann et al., Utah UP, 2020, pp. 106–16.

Getha-Taylor, Heather. "Leadership Across Hierarchical Levels." *Global Encyclopedia of Public Administration, Public Policy, and Governance*, edited by A. Farazmand, Springer, 2018, https://doi.org/10.1007/978-3-319-20928-9 _2208.

Griffin, Kimberly, et al. "Graduate Diversity Officers and Efforts to Retain Students of Color." *Journal of Student Affairs Research and Practice*, vol 53, 2016, pp. 26–38.

Grim, Jeffrey, et al. "The Experiences of Academic Diversity Officers at the University of Michigan." *Currents*, vol. 1, no. 1, 2019, pp. 1–20.

Hochschild, Arlie. *The Managed Heart: Commercialization of Human Feeling*. U of California P, 1983.

Hochschild, Arlie, and Anne Machung. *The Second Shift: Working Families and the Revolution at Home*. Penguin, 2012.

Liu, Helena. "Just the Servant: An Intersectional Critique of Servant Leadership." *Journal of Business Ethics*, vol. 156, 2019, pp. 1099–112.

Matthew, Patricia A., editor. *Written/Unwritten: Diversity and the Hidden Truths of Tenure*. U of North Carolina P, 2016.

Niemann, Yolanda Flores. "Want to Grow Women Leaders? Create the Pipeline Through Institutional Change." *Women Leading Change in Academia: Breaking the Glass Ceiling, Cliff, and Slipper*, edited by Callie Rennison and Amy Bonomi, Cognella Academic Publishing, 2020, pp. 301–19.

Niemann, Yolanda Flores, et al., editors. *Presumed Incompetent II: Race, Class, Power, and Resistance of Women in Academia*. UP of Colorado, 2020.

Pihakis, Jett, et al. *The Emergence of the Chief Diversity Officer Role in Higher Education*. Russell Reynolds Associates, 29 July 2019, https://www.russell reynolds.com/en/insights/reports-surveys/the-emergence-of-the-chief -diversity-officer-role-in-higher-education.

Settles, I. H., et al. "Scrutinized but Not Recognized: (In)visibility and Hyper-visibility Experiences of Faculty of Color." *Journal of Vocational Behavior*, vol. 113, 2018, pp. 62–74.

Stewart, Abigail, and Virginian Valian. *An Inclusive Academy: Achieving Diversity and Excellence*. MIT Press, 2018.

Whitaker, Manya, and Eric Grollman, editors. *Counternarratives from Women of Color Academics: Bravery, Vulnerability, and Resistance*. Routledge, 2019.

Williams, Damon A. "Seven Recommendations for Highly Effective Senior Diversity Officers." *Black Issues in Higher Education*, vol. 22, no. 7, 2005, p. 53.

— — —. *Strategic Diversity Leadership: Activating Change and Transformation in Higher Education*. Stylus Publishing, 2013.

Williams, Damon A., and K. C. Wade-Golden. *The Chief Diversity Officer: Strategy, Structure, and Change Management*. Stylus Publishing, 2013.

Worthington, R. L., et al. "Advancing the Professionalization of Diversity Officers in Higher Education: Report of the Presidential Task Force on the Revision of the NADOHE Standards of Professional Practice." *Journal of Diversity in Higher Education*, vol. 13, no. 1, 2020, pp. 1–22.

5

VALE LA PENA

Faculty Leadership and Social
Justice in Troubling Times

TANYA GONZÁLEZ

everal years ago, I was gifted a poster quoting Chicana scholar and activist Gloria Anzaldúa that reads, "Do work that matters; vale la pena." This poster hangs in my home office and serves as a backdrop to classes and meetings held remotely during the COVID-19 pandemic, reminding those who join me that working to make the world a better place matters. The full quotation from Anzaldúa's posthumously published *Light in the Dark/Luz en lo oscuro* reads, "May we do work that matters. Vale la pena, it's worth the pain" (22). Pain, sorrow, suffering, difficulty, and effort are all connoted in the word *pena*. When applied to the work that matters in institutions of higher learning, including social justice issues, Anzaldúa's words remind us that this is material *and* affective labor, and it is not easy or necessarily pleasant.

Campus leaders invested in diversity, equity, and inclusion efforts, regardless of their positions, know the difficulties faced on the paths toward changing a climate or culture. One perspective on the legacies of social justice work in higher education emphasizes the ways the development of ethnic and area studies and the implementation of multiculturalism, as well as social justice task forces, have operated as forms of containment (Ahmed, *On Being Included*; Walcott). Indeed, some have eloquently described how the eras of multiculturalism and diversity have done little more than contain difference and maintain the status quo in higher education. What these theorists see as the real problem is the entrenchment of systems that perpetuate white privilege, and to claim that the inroads in diversity since the twentieth century have or will dislodge those systems is a false reality. For instance, Rinaldo Walcott suggests "whiteness requires unmaking so that other possibilities for human life might emerge" (394). Others have argued that the structure of higher education is irreparable, calling for altogether alternative institutions (Harney and Moten). Walcott further explains,

> To claim that we can diversify, achieve equity, indigenize, or decolonize without taking on the social, cultural, political, and economic arrangements of whiteness is to enter the terrain of lies. [...] Such claims leave intact institutions not built for us, never meaning to receive us, as the ongoing regimen of our society. In essence, then, such appropriations of language invented to produce transformative change work to keep white supremacy intact even if it is an understated white supremacy. (398–99)

Walcott's pointed and bleak view of the reiteration of white supremacy via diversity work provides a response to the often-frustrating lack of substantive movement in terms of key goals for the recruitment, retention, and leadership development of Black, Indigenous, and People of Color (BIPOC) in the academy. It also provides a clear rationale for the resistance to support social justice-centered disciplines and departments, curriculum design, or employee trainings, despite stated institutional diversity goals.

Sara Ahmed uses the metaphor of the brick wall to describe the challenges of diversity work:

One of my primary aims has been to describe the physical and emotional labor of "banging your head against a brick wall." ... When you don't quite inhabit the norms, or you aim to transform them, you notice them as you come up against them. The wall is what we come up against: the sedimentation of history into a barrier that is solid and tangible in the present, a barrier to change as well as to the mobility of some, a barrier that remains invisible to those who can flow into the spaces created by institutions. (*On Being Included* 175)

The contrast Ahmed illustrates between a barrier to mobility for those who are outsiders and the invisibility of that barrier for those for whom the university was designed, forces us to grapple with the pain—the headache—that diversity work brings. As Ahmed further explains, when the system is designed for you, you can simply flow through the system, and you cannot see the real problems within it. Any articulation of those problems becomes a block to that flow, one that those who were moving nicely through then see as a problem or disruption or, generously I would add, a surprising revelation (Ahmed, *On Being Included* 186). Walcott's and Ahmed's realistic and accurate portraits of the structures of academic institutions contrast with Anzaldúa's call: "May we do work that matters: vale la pena, it's worth the pain." Walcott suggests the work may not matter, and Ahmed's apt wall cliché implies the pain may never cease, especially if those who comfortably exist within the university do not see the wall upon which one's head is banging, and thus wonder at the wails that come from every direction. However, a relationship between these two descriptions of social justice work, including diversity work in the academy, exists

This chapter brings these views together through the lens of my own leadership journey as a light-skinned, cisgender, first-gen, Latina, tenured professor of American Literature and Latinx studies; a leader of multiple faculty and staff affinity groups; the first Latina faculty senate president at my R1 institution; and most recently, as the chair of the university task force charged with evaluating faculty affairs policy through an anti-racist, social justice lens. This chapter reiterates the importance of recognizing the truth in these bleak descriptions of institutions of higher learning and the authors' acknowledgment that this view does not preclude action. Recognizing the pain and difficulties of this work, and choosing to remain in it, however, requires a belief that this work matters, that "we can make a positive difference for someone every day" (Niemann). As Laura Yakas writes in their response to Walcott's argument presented earlier, "When we accept this unacceptable world, we are more easily empowered to resist what we can resist, to take manageable bites out of the 'problem' of oppression, and commit ourselves to chewing forever" (Diaz et al. 384). In their optimism or in their realistic activism, these scholars believe leadership and social justice work matter and is worth the pain. This chapter explores how faculty leadership in turbulent times of social unrest, a pandemic, and attacks on faculty work requires the dual approach of seeing the truth of the situation and taking material action toward institutional adjustments and change that make these spaces a bit more tolerable. While these actions may not completely unmake the system to begin again from scratch, they are collaborative movements that can improve the structures and practices in place. Moreover, this chapter shows how we can learn from the past efforts of "unusual" leaders and how we might see in these activities the "misfit models" for reshaping higher education.[1]

SCRATCHES ON WALLS, MISFITS, AND QUEER USE

Anyone who has had to grapple with aging or inadequate laboratory space or other kinds of facilities on a university campus, like anyone who has spent time on home repair, understands the desire to tear down previous constructions and begin again. Starting from scratch can often

mean less expense and less effort than attempting to preserve or reproduce an old structure. To extend the comparison further, diversity work
in the current climate can feel like a never-ending episode of *This Old
House*, but instead of the army of contractors and construction workers and ample budget to restore the vitality and brilliance of the building, you have one paid expert, some volunteer laborers, and zero budget. While it is true that the genius configurations I have seen scientists,
engineers, and diversity workers create to account for inadequate resources often lead to entrepreneurial innovations and surprising produc-
tivity, the time it takes to accomplish goals is much longer than in fully
equipped endeavors. In this context, one has to wonder at the efficacy of
diversity work (Ahmed, *On Being Included*; Anderson; Flaherty; Harney
and Moten; Partridge and Chin; Walcott).

Returning to the question of the usefulness of trying to renovate
higher education in her provocatively titled *What's the Use?: On the Uses
of Use*, Sara Ahmed offers several metaphors for how institutions are,
or could be, shaped by diversity work.[2] Three of these tropes stand out:
scratches on walls, misfits, and queer uses. Ahmed returns to the image
of institutional brick walls and how useless it can seem to continue to
bump up against them. Identifying the walls against which one bumps,
whether through unofficial or official avenues of complaint, can make
them legible for those who are not affected by the difficulties or experiences they represent. The complaint serves as a mark on the wall, which
makes it legible in the present and into the future. Ahmed cleverly suggests complaints are signs or testimonies of collective resistance: "We
can reach each other through what appears as damage, mere scratch
and scribble. Complaints become writing on the wall: we were here;
we did not get used to it" (*What's the Use?* 217). Even if a complaint
is not resolved in the ways that we would want, Ahmed suggests the
act of complaining is worth the effort, especially as it connects future
students, staff, faculty, and administrators to a legacy of diversity work.
We can see examples of these "scratched walls" in collections such as

Presumed Incompetent and *Presumed Incompetent II*, which track narratives of women of color in higher education.

Writing on the walls of higher education marks the experiences of those who speak up about inequality on campuses. Ahmed calls these speakers the "misfits" who are called upon to serve institutions in part to avoid major protests, flare-ups, and disruptions on campus. She writes,

> Perhaps because organizations are trying to avoid such crises, misfits often end up on the same committees (otherwise known as the diversity committee). We might end up on the diversity committee because of whom we are not: not white, not cis, not able-bodied, not man, not straight. The more nots you are, the more committees you end up on! We can be misfits on these committees. (*What's the Use?* 172)

This last phrase can be read in two ways: that these spaces allow for misfit camaraderie *or* that we can represent another layer of misfitness even within a diversity committee. On the one hand, the university uses misfits to contain diversity work to particular committees and meetings; on the other, misfits remind us that containment is futile. Uniformity, consensus, and solidarity are not a given in these spaces. Intersectionality exists in layers of struggle that cannot be tidily packaged or encapsulated. As I will later show, whether found in diversity committees of various kinds or affinity group leadership, misfits produce "misfit methods" that are instructive as we lead diversity work from unusual leadership positions.

Whether volunteer students, staff and faculty labor, or administrative experts leading change, misfits often experience burnout when all they see is the scratches on the wall instead of more substantive efforts. Ahmed warns of this burnout and suggests that "queer use" is one strategy to avoid this fate: "We might have to mind the gap, as diversity workers, so we will not end up exhausting ourselves by bringing things into existence that do not come into use. But we can also *queer the gap*: by finding in the paths assumed to lead to cessation a chance of being in another way" (*What's the Use?* 208). When we are able to find and highlight different uses of existing systems, policies, organizations, and institutional structures organized by the majority, we can put what exists to shore up the exclusionary status quo to radically equitable use.

Of course, as Ahmed also notes, "Sometimes in order to survive institutions we need to transform them. But we still have to survive the institutions we are trying to transform" (*What's the Use?* 189). In what follows, I will trace some examples of reading and producing scratches on the walls, using misfit methods, and encouraging queer use that have led to work that matters at my institution.

WALL ART

For Ahmed, the scratches on the walls connect us to a legacy of complaint. I am fascinated with this idea because it imagines the ways institutional memory, history, and archival work can perform social justice. Several questions come to mind: Who is scratching the walls? How are these scratches presented? And how do they remain visible for future scratchers?

My initial visit to the campus where I earned tenure and promotion was during my job talk in the spring semester of 2005. Two components of my visit indicated to me that I might have found a work environment that cared about diversity, equity, inclusion, and belonging. The first was that my future department head had included a meeting with the president of the Latinx faculty staff affinity group in my visit itinerary. It was a short visit, but I was able to hear about the growing Latinx student population in Kansas, the history of affinity group presence and activism on campus, and the intersectional and international nature of these groups. In addition, there was a genuine sense that I could find professional success since this person was also a tenured professor and chair of the philosophy department in the same college I would enter. I would have a community with which to engage and collaborate on this campus. The impressions that I received from this exchange were re-affirmed during the tour with the research librarian dedicated to ethnic and gender, women, and sexuality studies. She showed me the "We Are the Dream" mural that had been created and dedicated in 1980 by the Black Student Union, Movimiento Estudiantil Chicano de Aztlán (M.E.Ch.A.), and Native American Indian Student Body. Given that I was terrified of moving from Southern California to Kansas alone, these moments and the material presence of civil rights heroes on the walls of the scholarly heart of the university indicated a legacy of work that I was interested in continuing and building on in my career. Just as Ahmed suggests that complaint can be the scratches on the wall, making these scratches visible in a recruitment process can serve as a reassurance that there may be space and potential for future wall art.

Of course, I was not totally naïve. Throughout my career, beginning as an undergraduate, I have benefited from myriad mentors and advocates who have made the scratches on the walls of the academy very clear.[3] I have always known that entering this space, even in the relative safety of an English department and as someone who also finds an interdisciplinary home in the fields of American ethnic studies and gender women and sexuality studies means participating as a misfit in the work of scholarship, teaching, and engagement within the university community and beyond. And being a misfit and scratching on the walls of higher ed takes a lot of time. Many others have documented the toll that identifying as an outspoken misfit takes on the areas of work that ensure tenure and promotion for faculty (Gutiérrez y Muhs et al.; Stewart and Valian).

That said, faculty and staff affinity groups, multicultural student groups, and diversity committees of all sorts also provide the community needed to survive the institutions that need transformation. My involvement with my local communities of misfits has taken time away from my scholarly pursuits, but it has allowed for collective action when the university has experienced overt white supremacy, blatant racism, attacks on immigrant groups, and lesbian, gay, bisexual, transgender, queer (LGBTQ)-phobia and aggressions, among other microaggressions. My involvement and support help mitigate the exhaustion of others and vice versa. While many diversity initiatives have been pushed for since I arrived on campus in 2005, it took sustained unusual leadership from traditionally marginalized alumni, faculty and staff groups, and the vocal complaints of students to see movement on these requests.

Making the scratches visible has meant marching. Making the scratches visible has meant writing and delivering speeches to thousands on campus, linking activist legacies to contemporary movements toward social justice and against the sustained destructive presence of white supremacy (González, "KSUnite Speech"). Making the scratches visible has meant students creating #blackatkstate. Making the scratches visible has meant a website documenting the progress of the strategic plan for a more inclusive university. Making the scratches visible has meant including folks with institutional memory at the table to know why particular policy language exists and how it comes into existence. Making the scratches visible means continuing to scratch, sometimes the same message over and over again.

The collective work of unusual or informal leaders—also known as "organizational catalysts," "grassroots leaders," and my favorite, "tempered radicals" (Stewart and Valian 432; Wambura and Hernandez 402–03)—combined with formal leaders committed to taking practical steps toward social justice, also coincided with the collective groans of global exhaustion with the violence against Black people, indigenous people, and other people of color. The success of these initiatives has depended on the solidarity between disparate groups and the constant reminder that what might be initially seen as wall scratches can also be understood as wall art that makes legible our voices and our presence. In 2020, my campus managed to build literal walls of a new multicultural student center founded on the spirit and legacy of generations of wall scratchers.

MISFIT METHODS

The misfit methods have been fierce and focused and grounded in continuing to make complaints visible *and* being strategic and flexible. As Ahmed notes, "When practitioners overcome resistance, it seems to reappear elsewhere. Institutional immobility thus requires a mobile defense system" (*On Being Included* 175). These communities of wall writers have actively registered complaints over the years, and my constant refrain as an informal faculty leader within these groups has been to encourage us to be solution driven. What do we need and want? And how can we form coalitions and partnerships to make that work happen? Of course, these strategies are founded in my scholarly training in women of color feminism and anti-racism theories of the 1980s and 1990s, which has been key in community organizing within the university. As Chela Sandoval writes,

> Differential technologies of oppositional consciousness, as utilized and theorized by a racially diverse U.S. coalition of women of color, demonstrate the procedures for achieving affinity and alliance across difference; they represent the modes that love takes in the postmodern world. The differential permits the generation of a new kind of coalitional consciousness and warrior-citizenship: countrywomen and countrymen of the same psychic terrain. (182)

The emphasis of my leadership within these groups has whenever possible (1) honored our intersectional experiences versus nationalist, ethnocentric, and sometimes sexist and LGBTQ-phobic positions, (2) encouraged coalitional coming together, (3) emphasized strategic mobility, and (4) looked toward material or measurable change. Emphasizing these steps has increased dialogue and action across campus, even expanding contributing to more involvement in shared governance, including resolutions that have been passed by the general faculty senate on support for Deferred Action for Childhood Arrivals students and more recently, social justice work, affinity group advocacy for the hiring of a vice president for diversity, equity, inclusion and belonging and the building of a multicultural student center, the development of a faculty senate social justice committee, curriculum reforms, and other initiatives.

The kind of informal leadership that I have engaged in throughout my career has been theorized and labeled by those studying diversity within the academy. Abigail Stewart and Virginia Valian have described in their study *An Inclusive Academy: Achieving Diversity and Excellence* that informal faculty leadership is enacted by those who "are respected on campus and have strong—even passionate—commitment to making a positive change. These individuals can play a critical role in initiating change and stimulating others—including formal leaders—to take on the issue they care about and institutionalize it" (432). Summarizing a 2011 study by Kezar and Lester, Stewart and Valian later list successful tactics for overcoming resistance or opposition to bottom-up change that resonates with what I see as misfit methods

> flying under the radar until there is evidence to support the change, creating internal and external networks, developing coalitions, obtaining allies in positions of power, recognizing and naming power dynamics, making modest changes in their proposals and reframing issues. They point out that formal leaders were almost always critical to the success of the efforts that began with informal leaders. (433–34)

My institution is fortunate that right now we have a provost and president who are openly supportive of social justice issues and initiatives on campus. They have appreciated, welcomed, and supported partnerships with informal leaders, shared governance, and their own teams, which has generated a lot of activity in these areas. Over the last five years, these collaborations have been crucial to the previously listed changes. As Stewart and Valian summarize, "Individuals can move beyond operating as persuasive experts and can foster institutional change when they are able to collaborate with formal leaders with access to formal institutional processes" (433). Interestingly, these misfit methods and moves toward a more just institution can have the most resistance from the general faculty. It can come as a shock to the system when they elect a misfit as faculty senate president.

I never dreamed I would serve as faculty senate president. I had served as a senator as an associate professor by filling the term of a senator who had left the university, and the curriculum and policy work was initially not compelling, especially since at the time I was serving as president of an affinity group and on multiple college- and university-wide hiring and diversity committees. In other words, I was doing informal faculty leadership work from the peripheries of official shared governance systems. In 2017, I was promoted to professor, and I began my first full three-year term as a faculty senator. This was also a particularly tumultuous year for the campus, as several anti-immigrant, nativist, and racist attacks shook the community. As administrative and programmatic responses to these events emerged, in particular the university president's canceling of classes and work for a campus-wide rally, faculty senate leadership realized that the faculty were not represented and requested a last-minute change to allow a senator to speak at the event. As a misfit senator, I was approached for the task. The first thing I did was gather the affinity group leadership so they could comment on a draft of my speech. Then I withheld the copy of my speech from the organizers to avoid any censorship.

Later that academic year, the same leadership team approached me to run for faculty senate president. When a colleague asked what my platform would be, I honestly replied that I didn't have one, except to continue working to make sure nobody gets treated badly. This remains my modus operandi as I transition from three years of service in faculty senate presidential roles to service as an interim associate provost. As Ngunjiri and Hernandez write,

By definition, tempered radicals are people who find themselves at odds with the dominant culture due to having different values and/or social identities (Mayerson, 2001). Tempered radical leadership is a critical change-oriented form of authentic leadership, whereby we utilize those multifocal lenses from our lived experiences and the fluidity of our identities as standpoints from which to lead. (402–03)

My leadership journey has centered on collecting the stories of my peers and colleagues, recognizing their needs, and working to facilitate the changes necessary to make our professional lives better. Here I agree with Anzaldúa's description of her project:

Mine is a struggle of recognizing and legitimizing excluded selves, especially of women, people of color, queer, and othered groups. I organize and order these ideas as "stories." I believe that it is through narrative that you come to understand and know your self and make sense of the world. . . . Your culture gives you your identity story, pero en un buscado rompimiento con la tradición you create an alternative identity story. (6)

These alternative identity stories that I have shared and experienced throughout my career have helped me situate myself and carve an authentic leadership style built on collective and coalitional power. While I may not have had the kinds of difficulties that many around me have suffered, I still operate from the standpoint that my knowledge of those hardships and pains requires me to act with those around me to improve things as we are able.

Not long into my year as faculty senate president-elect, I realized that one of the main issues that needed to be addressed on our campus was representation for term employees. While faculty senate leaders had been discussing this issue since the late 1990s, no movement had been made to change the situation. The past president had organized a faculty senate constitution committee to work through how this representation might look. What we faced throughout the discussions over the next year was a mistrust between college caucuses about how these new members would affect representation on the senate. No group wanted to lose votes on the senate, even when the numbers were not, as far as I could tell, significantly different from the current ratios. The national conversation on the need to include term employees in shared governance was plentiful, with good examples of how it could work. But as conversations continued, I became aware of growing mistrust in our process and the leadership. This would be a problem that I would inherit and not one I would solve, as the committee delved into more and more complex formulas for working through the issues. It took until the last month of my faculty senate leadership to see a proposal passed by the senate that provides term representation in the senate. While my misfit methods did not immediately succeed, they provided the foundation for change.

Continued action against social injustices, even within shared governance, has meant a mobile and strategic approach to working within the institutional system, especially since my tenure as faculty senate president happened to fall squarely during the COVID-19 pandemic. As Ahmed writes,

> For some, mere persistence, "to continue steadfastly," requires great effort, an effort that might appear to others as stubbornness, willfulness, or obstinacy.... Diversity work thus requires insistence. You have to become insistent to go against the flow, and you are judged to be going against the flow because you are insistent. A life paradox: you have to become what you are judged as being. (*On Being Included* 186)

I have the fortune to work with campus administrators who are invested in an inclusive academy and for whom my insistence has not been perceived as untoward but rather as a vital perspective with which to collaborate and lead. So as the pandemic closed campuses in March 2020, and we were tasked with facilitating academic continuity, I was comfortable making the case for swift policy adjustments, including a pause to tenure clocks, optional inclusion of teaching evaluations in review portfolios for 2020, and the inclusion of COVID-19 impact statements in faculty review.[4] Because our campus does not yet have a dedicated faculty affairs position within our provost's office, it has fallen to faculty senate leadership to partner with campus administrators to ensure academic continuity and that emergency management addresses faculty concerns. For this work, I was ever grateful for the faculty success listserv organized by the Association for Public and Land Grant Universities (APLU), as well as the ADVANCE network of professionals who were ready with researched and published information on which to base these immediate measures.

As on every campus, the speed with which we were called upon to modify our work caused massive stress. Our first weeks of remote work felt tumultuous, exacerbated by the realization of the seriousness and magnitude of the pandemic's effects on our lives. Following my misfit methods, I began an informal communication strategy of writing letters to campus as faculty senate president to communicate the radical care that leaders were taking for faculty, staff, and students and to express gratitude for the sacrifices of time and energy we were all making. These letters made efforts to show respect for faculty research and teaching, as well as the way various staff units were making herculean efforts to keep the university operational in radically different ways. I even released a video demonstrating the tragicomic realities of working from home with a seven- and four-year-old (González, "#kstatestrong"). The shift to online teaching and advising, the need to care for children or older relatives or partners at home, the financial stress of furloughs, and the disruptions to research, scholarship, creative activity, and discovery, as well as caring for our colleagues in distress created a surreal backdrop for leadership. But what came into focus was that misfit methods are inclusive; they can benefit everyone.

Of course, the pandemic was not the only issue that required attention throughout 2020. Budget shortfalls required various conversations with the administration, and I was tasked with leading several virtual town halls to present campus concerns to the administration. These dialogues were fruitful, even if mostly unsatisfactory, as initial guarantees to keep everyone employed through the 2019–20 academic year expired, and furlough planning and layoffs became realities as the academic term ended. The various communication platforms that I was able to publicly advocate for fair treatment of employees during these increasingly difficult times were no longer available as I turned over the presidency to a capable successor in June, but I remained active in the emergency management and academic continuity teams throughout 2020.

My first task as past president of the faculty senate in June 2020 was to establish an ad hoc committee on social justice to create consistent and sustained action plans for the faculty senate, in coordination with other campus entities: develop a syllabus statement on classroom conduct; review and revise the university policy prohibiting discrimination, harassment, sexual violence, domestic and dating violence, and stalking; review and revise the procedure for reviewing complaints; review and revise promotion and tenure, and grievance processes in light of best practices for diversity and inclusion; review the diversity curriculum requirement to ensure that anti-racism is addressed in all courses; protect free speech and civil discourse on campus and support clarifications in the student code of conduct and principles of community; review and revise policies governing student organizations to ensure that all recognized student organizations contribute to campus culture in a way that's consistent with our principles of community; work with other units on campus to develop anti-racism training for faculty and staff. Many of the items on this list also made it into the general plan for a more inclusive university, which has made visible the role of shared governance in contributing and leading in these efforts. In our charge, we also included a commitment for the faculty senate to work more closely with units engaged in social justice work, including the chief diversity and inclusion officer, the Diversity and Multicultural Student Affairs Office, and faculty staff affinity groups. The overt and sustained partnerships between these entities will hopefully ensure that the senate remains committed to material action in furthering these university goals.

QUEER USE

Scrutinizing and proposing adjustments to policy through a social justice lens requires a spirit of creativity, though in many ways this approach seems the least amenable to restructuring. In my experience, there is nothing more grounding than confronting a policy. By this I mean that a lofty goal can be grounded by the study of a policy and its needed changes. Policies are by their nature written to suggest fairness and equity, but they don't often work in that way for those in most need of the policies. As Ahmed adeptly states,

> A policy too can be a sign, a use instruction, a signaling of a direction. And a policy might be telling us that the university is open—that harassment will not be tolerated. A policy can be about what ought not to exist. The idea that something should not exist, or even that something does not exist because it should not exist, might be how something stays in use. I have observed that a policy can come into existence without coming into use. *Policies that are not in use can still be used as evidence of what does not exist.* Norms too can operate all the more forcefully by not appearing to exist. (*What's the Use?* 177)

As the current chair of a committee looking at our university promotion and tenure and grievance policies, this tension between policies and norms has come into sharp relief. In various instances as faculty senate president, I felt like I was making up problems and issues for us to solve. If that continues long enough, you can begin to inhabit the position of what Ahmed calls, the "wench in the works": "The 'wench in the works' has a queer kinship with the feminist killjoy—a kinship of figures can be a kinship of persons—as *nonreproductive agents*, as those who are trying to stop what usually happens from happening. A nonreproductive agent aims not to reproduce a line, not to follow in the footsteps of those who have gone before" (*What's the Use?* 213). Interestingly, when I learned more about what other institutions were doing to expand or adjust the ways they assessed faculty contributions to the work of the university, I began to see new paths that could better serve our faculty to measure how what they do aligns with stated university values, like engagement and diversity.

Often, the excitement one feels for new initiatives may not translate, especially for folks who are already doing a lion's share of the service work across campus. For instance, as faculty senate president, I charged the faculty affairs committee to expand our criteria for tenure and promotion review to include more language on internal and external engagement beyond that of the extension work we assess as part of our land grant mission. I also asked them to develop new criteria for teaching, research, professional, and public service activity that promotes diversity, equity, and inclusion. Despite the presence of our university's premiere expert on engagement, the team's questions made it clear that they were intimidated by the tasks or simply so stretched with service that the idea of this work was exhausting. In an effort to relieve their minds, I suggested that tackling one task and then later looking at another would be a good strategy. They agreed and accepted the task of looking at engagement. I began collecting information and examples for them, including an APLU report on the role of engagement in research that was distributed, but when COVID-19 hit, this work stalled.

In addition to pre-COVID service fatigue, this reticence hinted at the way we as faculty can become so used to a culture and the norms in which we exist that we do not see the need for policy to more clearly measure and give credit for the work we do. It also taught me that I should have followed my misfit methods more closely and come to the group with a solution—with language they could adjust versus creating from scratch, as it were. In response to Walcott and others' call to an entirely new structure, Gloria Diaz writes, "All of this is to argue that while radical solutions to issues of diversity and equality are necessary, the solutions should be mature, well developed, and realistic. . . . We have a responsibility to not burn ourselves or others out in the process to reach these goals and to make our goals realistic and beneficial in the largest ways" (Diaz et al. 387). The faculty affairs policy task force that I chair follows this advice, especially in the call not to burn ourselves or others out in the process of reaching our goals. We have scrutinized our current faculty handbook policies on faculty tenure and promotion and have noticed some policies not fully in use as well as other areas for development that resonate with the charge I gave the faculty senate group. However, this new group has recognized that in addition to adjusting and adding to policy, we need to spend more time on recommendations for department- and college-level practice, which seems to be the spot where the useful policies we have identified are not actually being used or followed. While there is still work to do on the policies, we know where we want to focus a major part of our collective energies.

In this strategy, we are engaged in what Ahmed calls queer use. As a reminder, Ahmed suggests that one strategy to avoid a loss of energy is to "*queer the gap*: by finding in the paths assumed to lead to cessation a chance of being in another way" (*What's the Use?* 208). We are looking within the policies that exist to find what is useful and equitable for those for whom the university was not built—for the many who are "not white, not male, not cis, not able-bodied, not man, not straight," and so forth (Ahmed, *What's the Use?* 172). Through my study of policy, for instance, I was able to suggest to our current faculty senate leadership that we could push for more equitable use of teaching evaluations across campus during the pandemic but also beyond that time. We needed to provide our colleagues the language that already existed in our faculty handbook that explicitly states that the evaluation of teaching shall not be exclusively conducted through student teaching evaluations but that other measures including peer reviews, teaching portfolios, the collection of syllabi, and professional development activity should be incorporated. This explicit language could empower faculty across the university to ask for more comprehensive evaluation, thus mitigating the effect of the bias that studies of student teaching evaluations have shown (Niemann 470, 492; Stewart and Valian 107, 145). Faculty senate leadership partnered with our teaching and learning center to put out a joint statement for campus prior to our last round of annual review.

Sometimes stopping the usual injustices from happening has less to do with fighting systems and more to do with knowing the systems in which one exists and guiding folks into more egalitarian and creative uses. What may have been produced to protect the status quo can actually serve to create safe practices for those for whom institutions were not built. There is something gratifying in finding within policy the language that encourages an entire community toward better ways of being. These instances accumulate to alleviate what most of us diversity workers feel much of the time—the exhausting weight of the dismantling and recrafting efforts. And this fact is what has helped me participate in this policy work with more attention and more care than I ever considered offering it before. We must not ignore the scratches that are staring us in the face. They may be evidence or clues that other scratchers may have visited this language before us. We can construct stories of those policymakers as diversity workers like us, though they may not have necessarily liked us.

One of the ways Ahmed uses the term *queering* is "being" another way and another is using things (paths, doorways, walls) another way from the way they were intended. This has been on my mind throughout this policy work. In addition to the more obviously useful policies, are there those that we can use in a different way than they were intended? In effect, this question slows me down because I begin to read in a "crafty" or creative way. In this kind of reading, I am following Ahmed's description of the queerness of use:

> To bring out the queerness of use requires more than an act of affir-
> mation: it requires a world dismantling effort. In order for queer use
> to be possible, in order to recover a potential that has not simply been
> lost but stolen, there is work to do. To queer use is work: it is hard and
> painstaking work; it is collective and creative work; it is diversity work.
> (*What's the Use?* 229)

Just because we find some of the policies useful, doesn't mean there isn't
more diversity work needed. We cannot become complacent about or
immune to the language of fairness that seems universal but creates no
way to move beyond inequity: "The very tendency to 'look over' how everyday and institutional worlds involve restrictions and blockages is how
those restrictions and blockages are reproduced. It is not the time to be
over it, if it is not over" (Ahmed, *On Being Included* 181). Those of us looking at the workings of institutions of higher education continue to do
work that matters, even when we review and craft policy. Attention to
this work makes a positive difference every day (Niemann).

CONCLUSION

Leaving scratches using misfit methods, and identifying and engaging queer uses exemplifies a persistence in effort despite recognizing
the realities of the situation. It is very clear that these scholar-activists
like Walcott and, especially, Ahmed, even in their scholarly inquiries
into diversity work, do not want diversity workers to quit the fight, no
matter how futile the longing for institutional dismantling and revolution may seem.

During 2020, the Kansas Board of Regents began investigating un-
derperforming programs across the regents' institutions, measuring
them in terms of numbers of majors and minors but not closely looking
at credit hour production or value to the mission of these institutions.

Even though my institution had one of the lowest number of programs under review, American ethnic studies and gender, women, and sexuality studies were held under scrutiny in a way that is hard not to interpret as ideological. Even when the provost made a case for their centrality to our work and that they served our diversity overlay and produced credit hours to sustain their size, the provost was charged with creating a plan to restructure. The resulting plan to combine the departments into a School of Social Justice is better than program closure, but such a demand from the Board of Regents forced immediate action without input or participation from the faculty in those programs, who then had to quickly find a way to reform.

On January 6, 2021, while insurgents and domestic terrorists attacked the Capitol Building in Washington, DC, the Kansas Board of Regents declared that their institutions would be able to shut down programs and fire tenured professors with thirty-day notice without declaring financial exigency (Garcia). While the regents provided forty-five days for institutions to provide a plan and required the plan to be made with shared governance, the move was rightly interpreted as a blatant attack on tenure and existing shared governance processes. The chief executive officers of every regents' institution, except the University of Kansas, declared that they would *not* use the regents' new policy but would rely on their existing processes to meet with the continued financial strain.

Kansas is not alone in these attacks on institutions of higher education. State legislatures across the country chose January 2021 to call for the elimination of tenure and other ideology-driven measures to chip away at academic freedom and the educational mission. Despite a new president of the United States, universities still grapple with white supremacy and racism, discriminatory policy, preserving access and democratic possibility, and helping their students ascertain truth from lies. As the United States reels from the attacks on the capital, we can see how our campuses have dealt with free speech and incendiary speech (Anderson). Collaborative on Academic Careers in Higher Education analysis indicates that universities have a long way to go to include BIPOC into universities from a sense of belonging and wouldn't recommend their institutions to other people of color (Flaherty). The Kansas Board of Regents' effort to provide more levers for its institutions of higher learning to grapple with dire financial circumstances epitomizes a vocal faction that chips away at academic freedom in the name of budgetary emergency.

Social justice work is never-ending, and faculty leadership can be an important voice of resistance in troubling times. After the 9/11 attacks, Anzaldúa wrote,

> As I see it, this country's real battle is with its shadow—its racism, propensity for violence, rapacity for consuming, neglect of its responsibility to global communities and the environment, and unjust treatment of dissenters and the disenfranchised, especially people of color. [. . .] Death and destruction do shock us out of our familiar daily rounds and force us to confront our desconocimientos, our sombras, the unacceptable attributes and unconscious forces that a person [culture/peoples] must wrestle with to achieve integration. (10, 16)

The same can be said about the loss of life from the authoritarian violence that Black people, Indigenous people, and other people of color have faced in the United States, whether through police brutality, other terrorisms, or the inequities in health and well-being that have been made more visible during the pandemic. Higher education is not immune to these issues and attacks. We are meant to tackle the world's big problems and train future leaders to care for others and think critically and creatively about the world around them, which requires us to confront our shadows.

Anzaldúa's words on the poster on my wall solidify the connections I see among various kinds of misfit diversity workers. An expansion of the quotation reads, "May we allow spirit to sustain and guide us from the path of dissolution. May we do work that matters. Vale la pena, it's worth the pain" (Anzaldúa 22). Her recognition of the paths falling apart and the need for sustenance and guidance to move forward is connected to spirit—a term that for Anzaldúa indicates a relationship with the intangible in the universe with which we *can* connect. While Anzaldúa's spirit is aligned with the traditional sense of animating life force, it also indicates energized vigor that emboldens us to move forward. It takes spirit to challenge the norms and status quo "paths of dissolution" so eloquently mapped out by theorists like Ahmed and later Walcott and others. And it takes spirit to sustain the creation of constructive paths through our institutions of higher learning. May we do work that materially, emotionally, psychically, holistically matters to the people who enter these spaces of higher education. "Vale la pena"; it's worth the effort and the pain.

NOTES

1. The term "misfit" is borrowed from Sara Ahmed's *What's the Use: On the Uses of Use* (172), and will be explained further below.

2. *What's the Use?: On the Uses of Use* is but one installment in a sustained, historically situated, and unapologetically realistic portrait of diversity work in higher education, which includes *On Being Included: Racism and Diversity in Institutional Life*, *Living a Feminist Life* (2016), and *Complaint!*

3. A very partial list of my professional mentors include (in chronological order of my meeting them) Drs. Susana Chávez-Silverman, Tiffany Ana López, Valarie Zapata, Orathai Northern, Traise Yamamoto, Amy Ongiri, Eliza Rodríguez y Gibson, Nicole Guidotti-Hernandez, Karin Westman, Michele Janette, Lisa Tatonetti, Rhondalyn Peairs, LaVerne Bitsie-Baldwin, Anita Cortez, Rebeca Paz, Kathy Green, Noel Schulz, Ruth Dyer (and other HERS alumna at my institution), Elena Machado Sáez, and the 2020 Wellesley HERS Cohort.

4. Though I presented the need for a COVID-19 impact statement, guidance, and recommendation to the faculty affairs committee in spring 2020, it did

not meet over the summer, so I worked on it with the associate provost and re-presented it to the committee in the fall 2020 semester. The document passed in the faculty senate in February 2021 and will be used in all faculty review processes until needed.

WORKS CITED

Ahmed, Sara. *Complaint!* Duke UP, 2021.

— — —. *On Being Included: Racism and Diversity in Institutional Life.* Duke UP, 2012.

— — —. *What's the Use? On the Uses of Use.* Duke UP, 2019.

Anderson, Greta. "A Fraught Balancing Act." *Inside Higher Ed*, 11 Jan. 2021, https://www.insidehighered.com/news/2021/01/11/colleges-weigh-taking -action-against-incendiary-comments-aftermath-capitol-attack.

Anzaldúa, Gloria E. *Light in the Dark: Luz en lo Oscuro: Rewriting Identity, Spirituality, Reality.* Duke UP, 2015.

Diaz, Gloria, et al. "Woke to Weary." *Public Culture*, vol. 31, no. 2, 2019, pp. 373–91.

Flaherty, Colleen. "Illusion of Inclusion." *Inside Higher Ed*, 6 Jan. 2021, https://www.insidehighered.com/news/2021/01/06/faculty-members-color-see -illusion-inclusion.

Garcia, Rafael. "A New Regents Policy on Firing Tenured Faculty Caught National Blowback, and KU is in the Crosshairs." *The Topeka Capital-Journal*, 7 Feb. 2021, https://www.cjonline.com/story/news/education/2021/02/07 /university-kansas-regents-ku-under-fire-policy-ignore-professor-tenure /4371953001/.

González, Tanya. "#kstatestrong." *YouTube*, uploaded 25 Mar. 2020, https:// www.youtube.com/watch?v=FQg6dNuB-Yk.

— — —. "KSUnite Speech." *YouTube*, uploaded 14 Nov. 2017, https://www.you tube.com/watch?v=2cgBde-IIIA.

Gutierrez y Muhs, Gabriella, et al., editors. *Presumed Incompetent: The Intersections of Race and Class for Women in Academia.* UP of Colorado, 2012.

Harney, Stefano, and Fred Moten. *The Undercommons: Fugitive Planning and Black Study.* Minor Compositions, 2013.

Niemann, Yolanda Flores. "Lessons from the Experiences of Women of Color Working in Academia." *Presumed Incompetent: The Intersections of Race and Class for Women in Academia*, edited by Gabriella Gutiérrez y Muhs et al., UP of Colorado, 2012, pp. 446–99.

Partridge, Damani J., and Matthew Chin. "Interrogating the Histories and Futures of 'Diversity' Transnational Perspectives." *Public Culture*, vol. 32, no. 2, 2019, pp. 197–214, https://doi.org/10.1215/08992363-7286777.

Sandoval, Chela. *Methodology of the Oppressed*. U of Minnesota P, 2000.

Stewart, Abigail J., and Virginia Valian. *An Inclusive Academy: Achieving Diversity and Excellence*. The MIT Press, 2018.

Walcott, Rinaldo. "The End of Diversity." *Public Culture*, vol. 32, no. 1, 2019, pp. 393–408.

Wambura Ngunjiri, Faith, and Kathy-Ann C. Hernandez. "Problematizing Authentic Leadership: A Collaborative Autoethnography of Immigrant Women of Color Leaders in Higher Education." *Advances in Developing Human Resources*, vol. 19, no. 4, 2017, pp. 393–406.

6

DISRUPTIVE AND TRANSFORMATIONAL LEADERSHIP IN THE IVORY TOWER

Opportunities for Inclusion, Equity, and Institutional Success

*PAMELA M. LEGGETT-ROBINSON AND
PAMELA E. SCOTT-JOHNSON*

The challenges that plague higher education can only be addressed through disruptive leadership. The acceptance of that disruption depends on the characteristics (race, gender, sexuality, economic and educational background) of the disruptor. While institutions currently embrace ideals of equity and inclusion, the person embodied in that *disruption* may find an unwelcoming environment. For example, the leadership offered by Black women is rejected, particularly as the system lacks authentic commitment to equity and inclusiveness. This chapter explores how Black women leaders negotiate the social and political structures in ways that disrupt the status quo and promote positive change. As we wrote this chapter, we drew on our, as well as others', personal experiences. Our commitment in writing the chapter is to make a difference as individuals who know the importance of voice and in *paying it forward*. Our organizational experiences, and those of others, are a paradox of knowing what to do and what is actually being done. We recognize the incongruity of knowing and doing. We do not write or share as victims or out of regrets but in knowing the potential sacrifices of speaking forthright and sharing our experiences to assist others. We want others to know that they are enough, and their gifts are to empower those around them from being their authentic selves. Furthermore, our critical lens of disruptive leadership is grounded in our lived experiences of intersectionality and the impact of the resulting engagements along our career trajectories. In addition, the lens we offer as Black women in higher education leadership is unique in that it offers new scholarship opportunities for what it means to be a disruptor (sacrificial) by the sheer nature of our existence and to disrupt systems that interfere with our ability to lead.

HISTORY OF HIGHER EDUCATION

American higher education was established from the wealth accrued through the Atlantic slave trade (Wilder). As such, the foundations were built on exclusion, separation, and privilege. Today, higher education is viewed as a necessary component of the nation's ideal of intellectual, social, and socioeconomic "opportunity." However, the "opportunities" afforded by higher education today, continue to exclude individuals based on gender, religion, race/ethnicity, and social class at every turn—recruitment, admissions, retention, and graduation. Lawrence and Keleher posit that the exclusionary practices continue in systems of hierarchy and inequity characterized by the preferential treatment, privilege, and power for white people at predominantly white institutions (PWI). PWI is the term used to describe institutions of higher learning in which Whites account for fifty percent or greater of the student enrollment. These institutions, both public and private, are understood to be historically white, were developed and rooted in the "binarism and exclusion supported by the United States prior to 1964" (Brown and Dancy; Williams) and operate in the same logic today (Wilder).

Covert racism facilitates the recurring preferential treatment and privilege of today's higher education, particularly in PWI. The elements of that covert racism are contextualized in access to knowledge (Wallenstein; Williamson), increased neoliberalism or market-driven policies and practices (Leal), and operationalized plantation politics (e.g., racist, colonial, and imperial epistemologies) for both students and faculty. Squire et al. define structural elements of higher education plantation politics as

- knowledge, or the beliefs of what is thought to be true;
- sentiment, or expressive feelings between two people;
- norms, or the rules that govern and control behavior;
- status, or the positions in a social unit;
- rank, or the arrangement of power into a social hierarchy;
- power, or the capacity to control others; and
- sanctions, or the allocation given based on conformity or non-conformity.

An ideal view of higher education is the opportunity to pursue *truth* through shared scholarship and verbal and written communications (Lemelle et al.). Thus, colleges and universities play an important role and responsibility in advancing these truths, and in some ways, advance equity in engaging in *truth telling*. However, despite improvements in educational equity since the 1950s, racial and gender discrimination for students, faculty, and leadership, continue to exist. Hensel reminded us of the historical structure of professorship as white male dominance and for which the curriculum was designed (e.g., disciplines, subjects, and topics of research) and contextualized (e.g., cultural views, beliefs, and norms).

"Professorships were originally designed for men who had wives at home not only to care for home and children but also to provide support for the man's career" (Hensel).

Although higher education has increased the number of diverse faculty over the past twenty years, white males continue to occupy fifty-three percent of full professors. Figure 6.1 demonstrates that Black and Hispanic women are more concentrated among the lowest ranks of the professoriate (*Condition of Education 2020*) and are promoted at a slower rate (Gregory). Incremental advancement within faculty ranks suggests the cultural environments of higher education institutions continue to perpetuate racial privilege through institutional practices, policies, and leadership.

HISTORY OF BLACK WOMEN IN HIGHER EDUCATION

The involvement of Black women in education in the United States can be dated as far back as slavery when enslaved women secretly learned to read and write. Although it was illegal for any slave to learn how to read or write, some female slaves had an infinite spirit of courage and jeopardized their well-being in efforts to teach other slaves to read and write (Wolfman). From the first admission into Oberlin College (Fletcher) to now, higher education continues to struggle to find ways to admit, retain, and graduate Black female students. The discriminatory practice of limiting or eliminating the access of Black women to colleges and universities created the establishment of Historically Black Colleges and Universities (HBCUs), with the first one in 1837. Although the existence of HBCUs offered opportunities for African American women to complete postsecondary studies, it was not until 1921 that an African American woman was able to earn a doctoral degree (Britton). To date, HBCUs have been successful in the recruitment, admissions, retention, and graduation of Black women from college, as well as the impact on the number of Black women obtaining graduate (MS, PhD) and professional degrees.

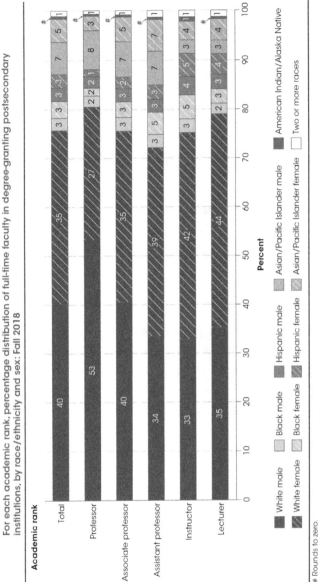

FIGURE 6.1 Academic ranks and distribution of full-time faculty, by gender, race/ethnicity, Fall 2018. (Source: *The Condition of Education 2020* [NCES 2020-144]. U.S. Department of Education, National Center for Education Statistics, 2020.)

LEADERSHIP IN THE ACADEMY

Definition of Leadership in Higher Education and Leadership Theories

Leadership is widely identified by theorists as a social influence process: essentially, change incidents in which an individual influences changes in others (Parry). Regardless of the organization, these theories define leadership as the art of motivating a group of people to act toward achieving a common goal. In order to understand leadership within the realm of higher education today, an exploration of leadership theories and models within higher education purported over time and across disciplines must be traversed. Additionally, it is important to note that leadership theories or models are not grounded in the framework of race or gender; both are leadership constructs developed by biases within higher education.

Bensimon et al. classified higher education leadership theories and models into six categories: trait theories, power and influence theories, behavioral theories, contingency theories, cultural and symbolic theories, and cognitive theories. These theories have been pared down from six traditional categories to four: trait, behavioral, contingency, and power and influence (Kezar).

- **Trait theories** identify specific personal characteristics that contribute to a person's ability to assume and successfully function in positions of leadership. This theory identifies identical traits for *all* leaders, transcending all contexts, and thus focuses their efforts on developing a definitive list of leadership traits (Bensimon et al.).
- **Behavioral theories** study leadership by examining the roles, categories of behavior, styles, and tasks associated with leadership and identifying tasks, such as planning, fundraising, or mentoring to understand leadership (Birnbaum, *How Academic Leadership Works*; Montez).

- **Contingency theories** emphasize the way situational factors affect leadership and explore different organizational subsystems, including the bureaucratic, collegial, political, and symbolic subsystems (Bensimon et al.; Birnbaum, *How Academic Leadership Works*).
- **Power and influence theories** consider leadership in terms of the source and amount of power available to leaders and the manner in which the leaders exercise that power, as well as the ability of leaders to use persuasion to achieve desired organizational outcomes (Fisher and Koch).

Transformational leadership theory is one of the most widely discussed and utilized theories that has risen to the forefront. It addresses current complex challenges within higher education and takes into consideration the full range of leadership capabilities (Avolio; Avolio and Walumbwa 331; Bass; Burns; Fusco et al.). Initially conceived as a process whereby leaders strategically transform the system or organization to a higher level by increasing the achievement and motivation of their followers, today, transformational leadership is defined as a leadership approach that causes change in individuals and systems (Litz and Blaik-Hourani). Transformational leaders work toward the benefit of the team, organization, and/or community; they are leaders focused on creating valuable and positive change in their followers by attending to the individual needs of followers, offering inspiration and motivation, and providing meaning to their work rather than just rewards.

Regardless of the leadership theory, effective leadership is central to an organization's success, and the calls for leadership to address challenges and opportunities are not new. Leadership effectiveness in higher education emanates from the need to bring together a multiplicity of stakeholders and is dependent upon institutional context (Osborn et al.; Ryan). That leadership imperative is grounded in achieving the vision and mission of academic excellence and significantly contributing to the national or regional economy through research, community, and intellectualism. Today's higher education leadership is multifunctional, multidimensional, and complex and involves managing through others and coping with change. It requires exploration through a systemic lens and a perspective that takes into account the intersection of relationships with regard to family, research, students, local communities, athletics, alumni, parents, media, public officials, faculty, and global interests.

At each societal turn, definitions of leadership and what it means to practice leadership in higher education are changing. However, leadership appointments are continually based on subject knowledge, experience on projects, and scientific accomplishments. Rarely are the appointments based on applicable leadership skills, as such, higher education falls short in building and supporting future academic leaders. Leadership development in higher education continues to be an under-investigated field of research and few studies investigate how or why faculty are appointed to leadership and how the challenges of complex and dynamic social, economic, and political contexts affect the appointment and retention for women.

Disruptive Leadership

Leadership plays a critical role in moving organizations to engage in essential "disruptive innovation" (Christensen et al., "Disrupting College"). The concept of disruptive leadership was inspired by Christensen's ("The Innovator's Dilemma") theory of disruptive innovation, which describes new technologies that upset and replace existing products. Although a formal definition of "disruptive leadership" does not exist, Ryan describes disruptive leadership as possessing the ability to deconstruct an existing norm or unsatisfactory status and examine the elements to determine that which is broken and, consequently, find a better way to rebuild a functional system or structure that better serves all stakeholders. This often means disrupting existing power structures to redistribute power and to encourage inclusivity by leading not from the top down but rather through emergent operating systems. Disruptive leaders do not seek recognition as leaders, nor do they seek to gain power.

Black women emerge from the perniciousness of higher education institutions as disruptive leaders. Their transcendence of racial and gender bias, stereotypes, and discrimination become the impetus for developing a disruptive leadership style. Black women often recognize and understand those solutions that are entrenched in societal, structural, and cultural hegemony. They approach solutions from a lens that identifies the complexity of wicked problems, plurality of stakeholders, and connectedness of the two. They are skilled in the art of negotiation of social, racial, and gender constructs; lead from their core values; and serve all stakeholders with empathy, humility, and grace. In higher education, disruptive leadership recognizes the need for courage in leading faculty into the future and transparency in addressing diversity, equity, and inclusion challenges. The disruptive leadership skills brought by Black women are needed for this new era, and, unfortunately, there is little acknowledgment for their successful skill set in higher education. Studies of Black women as disruptive leaders in higher education, however, are limited, thus revealing a need to investigate disruptive leadership practices by individuals who represent various dimensions of diversity and are influenced by factors such as gender or cultural background.

BLACK WOMEN IN LEADERSHIP

Leadership development rarely accounts for nor leads to leadership appointments for women in higher education. Thus, conversations regarding the lack of diverse leadership and the continuing myth that men are better leaders than women plague higher education and serve to stifle leadership ascension. Although studies within the last two decades show women earn the majority of postsecondary degrees and outperform men on numerous leadership competencies (Madsen, "Why Do We Need More Women"), the number of women in leadership positions (e.g., deans, vice presidents, provosts, or chancellors) is not reflective of the research (Carter and Wagner 1; Woolley et al.). Conversely, the fact that white women hold 26.4% of president, provost, and chancellor positions and Black women represent a mere 4.5% of these same positions indicates the unequal status of Black women compared to their white and male counterparts in university leadership positions (Gallant; Mainah and Perkins). This continued underrepresentation of women in leadership has a detrimental effect on the institutions themselves and the communities served. More importantly, the "lack of" shapes student perspectives and ambitions of leadership for future generations. To this end, scholars continue to emphasize the need for more Black women to be developed for leadership roles, as well as the importance of having a greater diversity of leadership in higher education (Madsen, "Women and Leadership").

As research continues to highlight the need for leadership inclusivity, it is essential to acknowledge and remember how gender plays a key role in leadership ascension, appointment, and retention. By essential and conventional definitions and associations with power, patriarchy, and hegemonic masculinity in higher education, traditional concepts of leadership present particular challenges for women in formal and informal leadership roles. Thus, the progression of women toward leadership positions in higher education is a complex and multifarious process (Johnson et al.).

The introduction of race to women's leadership shifts the conventional perception of "gender-driven leadership" into racially driven stereotypical roles (Ifeanyi). Just as research has not adequately accounted for the role of intersectionality (the combined oppressive system of race and gender) in faculty hiring, appointments, or retention, the same case can be made for higher education leadership. According to Ifeanyi, leadership in higher education is typically associated with white men, Black men, and white women, respectively. When higher education contemplates leadership, Black women are seen as unqualified; their psychosocial attributes and social and cultural aspects are considered to be problematic and outside the normative view of the leadership circle of higher education.

Organizational policies, practices, and processes continually perpetuate inequality and prejudice leading to the glass ceiling effect for women. The term *glass ceiling* portends to describe the ascension progress for women in higher education leadership. The progression of reaching top executive positions is due to the cultural and often impermeable barrier grounded in gender disparities for white women and both race and gender disparities for Black women (Baxter and Wright; Liggins-Moore; Merchant). White women describe these various experiences as blocking their career advancement. Black women, who face more difficult challenges, describe the *glass ceiling* as a *concrete ceiling* (*Advancing*). The metaphor of a concrete ceiling positions itself in sharp contrast to that of the glass ceiling, which one can actually see through. The *concrete ceiling* limits access to leadership positions for Black women because of the limited number of mentors or sponsors, lack of information and difficulty networking with influential colleagues, few role models who are members of their racial or ethnic group, stereotype threat, discrimination, and lack of high visibility assignments (Beckett; Davidson; Pierre).

Regarding privilege, Black women seeking leadership positions have unique challenges compared to their white and/or male peers. For example, because Black women are neither male nor white, they do not have access to the privileges inherent in male and/or white group membership (McIntosh). Additionally, Black women face a type of double jeopardy, encompassing both feminine interpersonal qualities, such as collaboration and cooperation, and masculine qualities, such as assertiveness and self-assurance, again giving rise to the notion of being neither white nor male (Carter). Lastly, the intersection of both race and gender, which cannot be separated for Black women, factors into leadership progression. Neither male nor white group members simultaneously own these physical characteristics and thus are able to experience a level of "privilege" within higher education leadership. Opportunities for advancement for Black women to leadership positions have increased; however, a deeper level of exclusion continues to persist.

BLACK WOMEN LEADERSHIP AT HISTORICALLY BLACK COLLEGES AND UNIVERSITIES (HBCUS)

Education has been the epicenter of the Black community since emancipation, with many institutions of higher learning built on the backs of enslaved Blacks (Poon). The attainment of education has always been deemed as respectable and as a means of uplifting the African American community (Wallace et al.). However, the doors to education, especially higher education, have not always been open for Black women (Abelman and Dalessandro; Parker; Wallace et al.). HBCUs are Black academic institutions whose principal mission was, and is still, the education of Black Americans.

Today, public HBCUs continue to produce talent for the twenty-first century with a disproportionate number being young women. Although Black female students make up most of the student body, faculty and administration at HBCUs still represent a male-dominated world, and female professors at HBCUs experience discrimination in pay and in position (Bonner). Therefore, gender is not only an issue that needs to be addressed with regard to the students at HBCUs but also an issue that is affecting the faculty at HBCUs (Gasman et al.).

Prototypes of leaders are predominantly male, even in the contexts where women faculty and students outnumber men, such as HBCUs, minority-serving institutions (MSIs), and small liberal arts institutions, as well as education, social sciences, and communication units. Masculine discourse dominates institutions, and white hegemonic structures continue to occupy the majority of senior positions and determine merit definitions, values, and norms that discriminate against Black women while inciting privilege for Black men. Even at MSIs, collective conceptions about leaders and leadership perpetuate the preference for men or women and continue to reinforce traditional, outdated, nonfunctional, and nonprogressive leadership and leadership models.

According to Bonner, HBCU faculty women were less likely to be tenured (37.1% to 43.4% for men) and less likely to hold the ranks of professor (33.7% to 46.8%) or associate professor (29.0% to 33.6%). Like women in PWIs, women on the tenure track at HBCUs were more likely (16.6% to 11.5%) to be among the lower ranks (e.g., nonacademic ranked instructors and lecturers; Bonner). Even more disparaging are the numbers of Black women in leadership positions at HBCUs who fail to progress to key leadership positions. These women remain last on the list of appointees and fall behind Black and international men. However, within the last ten years, Black women have shattered stereotypes and excelled in key campus leadership positions across the academic enterprise. Among the nation's 101 HBCUs, twenty-two Black women serve as presidents. Conversely, Black men still lead the larger, more prestigious HBCUs (Bonner).

BLACK WOMEN AND THE PRESIDENCY IN HIGHER EDUCATION

Leadership positions in higher education vary from department chair, dean, provost, vice president, chancellor, and/or presidency. The route in which one progresses also varies based on the institution, position availability, and sponsorship. However, many women, regardless of race and ethnicity, serve as department chairs or deans. Black women fail to progress to the levels of provost or chief academic officer or to the presidency at the same rates as Black men and white women. According to the American Council of Education (ACE), the percentage of minority college presidents increased slowly over the last thirty years, with numbers for Black women remaining disproportionately low compared to Black men and white women (figures 6.2 and 6.3). The few Black women serving as college presidents do so at MSIs (i.e., HBCUs). According to a 2017 report by ACE, the number of university presidents and chancellors was almost five times for white males than for minority males. The same report indicated that there were five times the number of presidents and chancellors for white women than for minority women (table 6.1).

TABLE 6.1 Comparison of College Presidents by Gender and Race/Ethnicity (%)

YEAR	MINORITY MEN	MINORITY WOMEN	WHITE MEN	WHITE WOMEN
2016	12	5	58	25

Source: American Council on Education.

One area in leadership that has not received attention is the homogenization of the term *Black* to encompass both foreign-born and native-born Black persons. The term *Black* is used without fully examining the cultural differences between the two groups nor investigating their response to leadership attainment and adversity (Leggett-Robinson et al.). To gain a true analysis of the number of Black women (native born) in leadership, researchers must disaggregate the data. These trends are consistent, with Black administrators continuing to be disproportionately underrepresented in comparison to their white counterparts (Valverde). Figure 6.2 shows there has been little to no increase since 2001 in the number of *Black* serving at the highest levels of institutional leaders (i.e., presidents or chancellors). In figure 6.3, the trend suggests that while the numbers of Black female presidents have increased since 2001, those gains are marginal relative to the overall numbers of presidential/chancellor positions. Likewise, the number of Black male presidents is decreasing.

HIGHER EDUCATION TODAY AND THE NEED FOR DISRUPTIVE LEADERSHIP
Higher Education Today

For over two hundred years, higher education has been viewed as a societal good, a public service. More specifically, the goal of higher education has been to prepare graduates for the demands of society, to prepare minds that can contribute to improving the human condition, and

College Presidents, by Race/Ethnicity

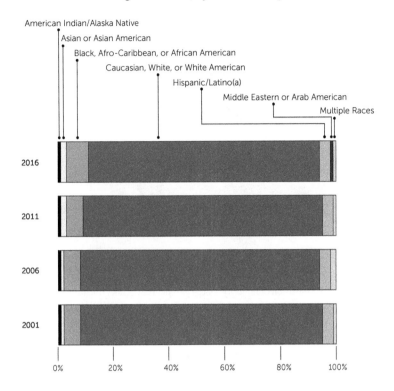

2016
American Indian/Alaska Native: 1%
Asian or Asian American: 2%
Black, Afro-Caribbean, or African American: 8%
Caucasian, White, or White American: 83%
Hispanic/Latino(a): 4%
Middle Eastern or Arab American: 1%
Multiple Races: 1%

2006
American Indian/Alaska Native: 1%
Asian or Asian American: 1%
Black, Afro-Caribbean, or African American: 6%
Caucasian, White, or White American: 86%
Hispanic/Latino(a): 4%
Middle Eastern or Arab American: 0%
Multiple Races: 2%

2011
American Indian/Alaska Native: 1%
Asian or Asian American: 2%
Black, Afro-Caribbean, or African American: 6%
Caucasian, White, or White American: 87%
Hispanic/Latino(a): 4%
Middle Eastern or Arab American: 0%
Multiple Races: 1%

2001
American Indian/Alaska Native: 1%
Asian or Asian American: 1%
Black, Afro-Caribbean, or African American: 6%
Caucasian, White, or White American: 87%
Hispanic/Latino(a): 4%
Middle Eastern or Arab American: 0%
Multiple Races: 1%

FIGURE 6.2 Comparison of college presidents by race (%). American Indian/Alaska Native, Asian or Asian American, Black, Afro-Caribbean, or African American, Caucasian, White, or White American, Hispanic/Latino(a), Middle Eastern or Arab American, Multiple Races. (Source: American Council on Education, *American College President Study 2017*, https://www.aceacps.org/.)

College Presidents, by Gender: Black, Afro-Caribbean, or African American

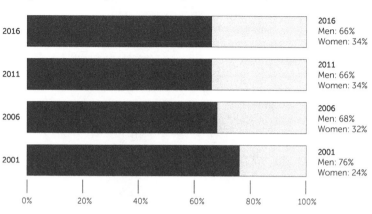

FIGURE 6.3 Comparison of minority college presidents by gender (%). (Source: American Council on Education, *American College President Study 2017*, https://www.aceacps.org/.)

to prepare individuals for the vast array of workplace demands required of future generations. It does so through opportunities and activities that inspire critical thinking, civic involvement, realization of passions, and personal development.

Historically, higher education was developed for white men; however, the landscape has changed. Today, women earn almost sixty-two percent of all associate degrees, fifty-eight percent of bachelor's degrees, sixty percent of master's degrees, and almost fifty percent of legal and medical degrees (King and Gomez). According to these researchers, women have not only made significant inroads in securing postsecondary degrees but there has been constant growth in the number of women securing full-time faculty positions as well. What has not changed is the leadership in higher education. From the lens of race or gender, the landscape is the same. Nationally, about eight percent of college administrators (department chairs, deans, student affairs, and vice provosts) are Black. These changes remain nominal since researchers started tracking the data in the 1980s (Stirgus). Conversations are taking place all over the country to address diversity in higher education executive leadership. For example, a report by the *Atlanta Journal-Constitution* (Stirgus) identified a mismatched alignment of diverse student demographics and leadership (table 6.2). Regarding leadership attributes, the needle has moved slightly from traditional "top-down" authoritative styles to more transformative leadership styles.

Additionally, the challenges of higher education have changed within the last ten years. In 1948, Einstein wrote, "Our situation is not comparable to anything in the past. It is impossible, therefore, to apply methods and measures which at an earlier age might have been sufficient" (Ryan). This observation holds true as the complexity of today's educational disparities and societal problems. Problems that are more recent include changes in state commitments to education, which have led to declines in state funding. Other issues that plague higher education are the consumer values related to the devaluation of liberal arts education and consumer-like demand for return on investment. The decline in budgets impacts faculty hires, with increases in noncontingent and part-time, nontenured, adjunct faculty. The use of technology as a learning platform certainly has added to the complexities of higher education. Finally, the changes in student demographics and student learning styles have brought new challenges that call into question the traditional existence of higher education (Buskirk-Cohen et al.; Pucciarelli and Kaplan).

Fast-paced, data-driven models for scientific research, the need for civil and inclusive working environments, and better, more transparent communication at all levels of the organization are driving how students are being educated and systems are being led. Furthermore, changes in student demographics have major impacts on how higher education approaches social justice on its campuses (Morreale and Staley; Selingo). These challenges are actually disruptions to traditional higher education and cause leaders to rethink everything from the delivery of education, to finding new revenue streams. Other ways in which current leaders must rethink their roles are in providing students with measurable outcomes that align with the marketplace, refining faculty

TABLE 6.2 An Example of the Mismatched Alignment of Diverse Student Demographics and Leadership Identified in an _Atlanta Journal-Constitution_ Article

Four of Georgia's academic institutional leadership (e.g., deans, provost, vice presidents, and presidents) fail to reflect the students attending those universities

INSTITUTION (PUBLIC) AND CARNEGIE CLASSIFICATION	ADMINISTRATORS % WHITE	ADMINISTRATORS % BLACK	ADMINISTRATORS TOTAL	STUDENT POPULATION % WHITE	TOTAL MINORITY STUDENT POPULATION %*
University of Georgia (Flagship; R1)	81.5	6.0	232	67.2	32.8
Georgia State University (Urban & MSI; R1)	71.1	17.8	45	27.7	72.3
Georgia Tech (R1)	74.6	14.3	63	47.1	52.9
Augusta University (RM)	87.5	12.5	32	54.9	45.1

Data source: _Data USA_ (https://datausa.io/) and Stirgus.

*Total minority student populations = Black, Hispanic, Asian, American Indian or Alaska Native, Native Hawaiian or Other Pacific Islander, and Ethnicity Unspecified; R1= highest research activities; RM = research and medical school.

workforce to address cost-cutting, and coping with the emerging educational needs of a new generation of students. Finally, today's leadership must seek ways to eradicate institutional and structural racism (Thompson and Miller). Plainly speaking, today's successful leaders must "disrupt" dysfunctional social and higher educational systems and offer alternatives that better serve stakeholders.

The Need for Disruptive Leadership

Several paradigm shifts are central to the changing context and increased demands within higher education. These demands include (1) inclusivity in pedagogy, (2) student and faculty demographics, (3) differentiated learning platforms, and (4) nontenure-track academic workforce. Institutions of higher education are often too committed to existing paradigms, traditional populations, and are usually unwilling to pursue new and/or niche markets (Birnbaum, "The Innovator's Dilemma"), thus overlooking innovations "outside of normal management and value frameworks" to reposition themselves. Homer-Dixon developed the concept of the "ingenuity gap" that exists when a society cannot supply sufficient ingenuity to meet its need to solve problems. The two types of ingenuity are technical and social. Technical ingenuity is used to create new technologies that help to solve problems in the physical world. Social ingenuity helps to solve the problems of the social world (i.e., social injustices). The changing context and increased demands in higher education, combined with a highly constrained resource environment and the ingenuity gap, has created a climate tailor-made for disruptive leaders (Wildavsky et al.). Most importantly, disruptive leadership is a necessary and adaptive response to the increasing complexity of problems, the pace of change, and globalization.

Disruptive Leadership Strategies for Black Women

While there is limited research on Black women as disruptive, higher educational leaders, many Black women use their daily personal and professional lives to navigate the social and political structures to address the challenges of today's higher education landscape. Disruptive leaders use contradictory tactics such as scaling across and translocal learning by recognizing that solutions, services, and products cannot be a one-size-fits-all approach, particularly in a rapidly changing and complex world. Translocal learning requires carrying ideas and solutions from one community to another, while adapting, evolving, and growing in ways that are conducive to that particular community or institutional setting (Ryan). These leaders must demonstrate courage, take risks, create a visionary narrative for the future, engage collective energy, reframe problems while offering opportunities, and provide alternatives to a broader audience that is increasingly underserved, first-generation, and ethnically and culturally diverse. More importantly, these leaders must intentionally cultivate new ideas and disrupt nonfunctioning, nonequitable systems.

BLACK WOMEN AS DISRUPTIVE LEADERS IN HIGHER EDUCATION

Leadership matters, but the ease which Black women lead may be perceptually different based on the intersection of gender and race. Despite efforts of diversity and inclusion, the academy continues to favor white men and women, especially in the vein of leadership and its "white power" cultural traits. These traits influence not only paradigms of leadership but also set general expectations of leadership behavior, style, and communication. When Black women enter the leadership arena, their actions and words are judged through the cultural lens of white privilege. Black women's passion and enthusiasm are often described as angry, assertive, aggressive, passionate, and emotional. All of which are counter to the cultural traits described for white men or white women in leadership roles.

Researchers separate leadership theories and characteristics and make assumptions that one is better than or favored over the other. We posit, however, that the combination of disruptive and transformational leadership skills is needed for today's higher education institutional success. Although the fundamental distinction between transformational and disruptive leadership is intent, intention does not have to occur simultaneously. Transformational leadership is the ability to articulate a vision and the ability to inspire followers, while disruptive leadership is concerned with the empowerment of others through organizational structures. Thus, to transform, disruption must first occur.

Today's challenges require a leadership style that addresses the wide range of complex and wicked problems plaguing both society and higher education institutions. These, much needed, leaders are typically packaged in the body of Black women. Regardless of their nontraditional package, Black women know that leadership ascension and survival in the academy is not an "academic" skill; it is a learned behavior. This learned behavior is grounded in the framework of constructivism, intersectionality, and disruption, and by all intents and purposes, it is not only transformative but also manifests itself as long-term institutional success.

For Black women in the academy, the constructivist framework equates to "controlling their own leadership learning"—that is, seeking outside professional development opportunities, investigating integrative approaches of their own professional effectiveness, and using evaluative tools of self-reflection and introspection to ultimately assess their own leadership development. Furthermore, the constructivist approach affords Black women an opportunity to become agile in situational awareness, stakeholder engagement, connective awareness, and reflective judgment.

Black women lead from the intersection of race and gender. Although not typically considered a privilege, intersectionality favors Black women in this case for disruptive leadership. As neither race nor gender can be separated for Black women, they are keenly equipped with a deep understanding of the complex socially guided perceptual, interactional, and micropolitical activities that seek to keep the status quo in higher education, thus limiting leadership ascension and stagnating opportunities for those outside the higher education circle (West and Zimmerman). The lived experience of intersectionality gives rise to the foundational desires of disruptive leadership: (1) challenge hegemony, (2) include voices from the periphery, and (3) engage in disruptive wonder (questions and reassess the social constructs beneath the problem).

More importantly, intersectionality, from the lens of disruptive leadership, positions Black women to be successful, transformative leaders in higher education. To gain additional understanding of Black women and disruptive leadership, the authors interviewed several Black women in leadership positions. The responses highlight leadership styles that contribute to the achievement and advancement of Black women despite barriers faced on their journey to executive leadership. Most of these women describe their leadership styles as transformational, while fewer describe themselves as servant leaders.

The responses revealed gender bias, discrimination, tokenism, and microaggressions—challenges that still exist in higher education. However, these challenges were overcome through these respondents' resilience, strategic thinking, commitments, and integrity. The commonalities for overcoming many of the leadership challenges were relationships with strong mentors, resilience, and collaborations. The respondents describe their leadership style as transformational or servant. Interestingly, none of the respondents described their leadership style as disruptive. As the term *disruptive* can insinuate a negative connotation, it may have been best to define disruptive leadership within the context of the survey.

SUGGESTIONS FOR PRACTICE
AND RESEARCH (CLOSING THOUGHTS)

Studies of disruptive leadership are limited, especially those investigating Black women. Additionally, theoretical studies that are grounded in leadership and specifically in disruptive leadership are not available. To build upon this foundation, further research could explore the following:

1. What avenues of inquiry could be explored to further understand the phenomenon of disruptive leadership for Black women?
2. What factors that contribute to Black women's self-development as leaders would be of value to those tasked with preparing future leaders?
3. How does intersectionality impact the development of disruptive and transformational leadership strategies for Black women?

SUMMARY/CONCLUSIONS

Advancing Black women in leadership roles benefits institutions, as it increases the number and variety of role models available to both faculty and students. Significant gains for institutions with Black women at the helm could disrupt structural and dysfunctionality embedded in higher education. Black women's leadership could also help address, and potentially eliminate, many of the challenges (e.g., funding declines, contingent faculty; increased use of technology; consumerism; changing demographics) in higher education. Black women, through their lived personal and professional experiences, are equipped to address other higher education challenges like social justice, gender pay and opportunity equity, diverse practices and perspectives in leadership, and inclusive behaviors (Patton). Finally, greater diversity in higher education leadership could better address long-standing issues, such as helping the increasing percentage of low-income and first-generation students in colleges earn degrees and enter the workforce or graduate/professional schools.

WORKS CITED

Abelman, Robert, and Dalessandro, Amy. "The Institutional Vision of Historically Black Colleges and Universities." *Journal of Black Studies*, vol. 40, no. 2, 2009, pp. 105–34.

Advancing African American Women in the Workplace: What Managers Need to

Know. Catalyst, 2004, https://www.catalyst.org/research/advancing-african
-american-women-in-the-workplace-what-managers-need-to-know/.

American Council on Education. *American College President Survey 2017,* https://
www.aceacps.org/.

Avolio, Bruce. *Full Leadership Development: Building the Vital Forces in Organization.* Sage Publications, 1999.

Avolio, Bruce, and Fred Walumbwa. "16 Authentic Leadership Theory, Research
and Practice: Steps Taken and Steps That Remain." *The Oxford Handbook of
Leadership and Organizations,* edited by David V. Day, 2014, p. 331.

Bass, Bernard M. *Transformational Leadership: Industrial, Military, and Educational Impact.* Lawrence Erlbaum Associates, 1998.

Baxter, Janeen, and Erik O. Wright. "The Glass Ceiling Hypothesis: A Com-
parative Study of the United States, Sweden, and Australia." *Gender and
Society,* vol. 14, no. 2, 2000, pp. 275–94, https://doi.org/10.1177/0891243000
14002004.

Beckett, Mary. *A Phenomenological Qualitative Study on the Concrete Ceiling for
Women of College in the Workplace.* 2020. University of Phoenix, PhD dissertation. *ProQuest,* https://search.proquest.com/openview/1864742c31ba1f86
c7c1e8b64c87fbf5/1?pq-origsi.

Bensimon, Estela M., et al. *Making Sense of Administrative Leadership: The "L"
Word in Higher Education.* ASHE-ERIC Higher Education Report No. 1
ED 316 074 MF-01. George Washington University, 1989.

Birnbaum, Robert. *How Academic Leadership Works: Understanding Success and
Failure in the College Presidency.* Jossey-Bass, 1992.

— — —. "The Innovator's Dilemma: When New Technologies Cause Great
Firms to Fail/the Innovator's Solution: Creating and Sustaining Successful
Growth." *Academe,* vol. 91, no. 1, 2005, 80–84.

Bonner, Florence. "Addressing Gender Issues in the Historically Black College
Community: A Challenge and Call to Action." *Journal of Negro Education,*
vol. 70, no. 3, 2001, 176–91.

Britton, Lois M. *African American Women in Higher Education: Challenges En-
dured and Strategies Employed to Secure a Community College Presidency.* 2013.

National-Louis U, PhD dissertation, https://digitalcommons.nl.edu/diss/68.

Brown, M. Christopher, and T. Elon Dancy. "Predominantly White Colleges and Universities." *Encyclopedia of African American Education*. Vol. 1, edited by Kofi Lomotey, Sage Publications, 2010, pp. 523–26.

Burns, James MacGregor. *Leadership*. Harper & Row, 1978.

Buskirk-Cohen, Allison A., et al. "Using Generational Theory to Rethink Teaching in Higher Education." *Teaching in Higher Education*, vol. 21, no. 1, 2016, pp. 25–36, https://doi.org/10.1080/13562517.2015.1110787.

Carter, Deborah. "Double Jeopardy: Women of Color in Higher Education." *The Educational Record*, vol. 68, 1988, pp. 98–103.

Carter, Nancy M., and Harvey M. Wagner. *The Bottom Line: Corporate Performance and Women's Representation on Boards (2004–2008)*. Catalyst, 2011, https://www.catalyst.org/knowledge/bottomline-corporate-performance-and-womens-representation-boards-20042008.

Christensen, Clayton M. *The Innovator's Dilemma: When New Technologies Cause Great Firms to Fail*. Harvard Business School Press, 1997.

Christensen, Clayton M., and Henry J. Eyring. *The Innovative University: Changing the DNA of Higher Education from the Inside Out*. Jossey-Bass, 2011.

Christensen, Clayton M., et al. *Disrupting College: How Disruptive Innovation Can Deliver Quality and Affordability to Postsecondary Education*. Center for American Progress, 2011, https://files.eric.ed.gov/fulltext/ED535182.pdf.

The Condition of Education 2020 (NCES 2020-144). U.S. Department of Education, National Center for Education Statistics (NCES), 2020.

Davidson, Marilyn. *The Black and Ethnic Minority Woman Manager: Cracking the Concrete Ceiling*. Sage Publications, 1997.

Fisher, James L., and James V. Koch. *Presidential Leadership: Making a Difference*. Oryx Press, 1996.

Fletcher, Robert Samuel. *A History of Oberlin College from Its Foundation Through the Civil War*. Oberlin College, 1943, http://books.google.com/books?id=ivcDAQAAIAAJ.

Fusco, Tony, et al. "Can Coaching Psychology Help Develop Authentic Leaders? Part Two." *The Coaching Psychologist*, vol. 7, no. 2, 2011, pp. 127–31.

Gallant, Andrea. "Symbolic Interactions and the Development of Women Leaders in Higher Education." *Gender, Work & Organization*, vol. 21, no. 3, 2014, pp. 203–16.

Gasman, Marybeth, et al. "Gender Disparities at Historically Black Colleges and Universities." *Higher Education Review,* vol. 47, no. 1, 2014, pp. 56–76, http://repository.upenn.edu/gse_pubs/351.

Gregory, Sheila T. "Black Faculty Women in the Academy: History, Status and Future." *The Journal of Negro Education*, vol. 70, no. 3, 2001, pp. 124–38.

Hensel, Nancy. *Realizing Gender Equality in Higher Education: The Need to Integrate Work/Family Issues.* ASHE-ERIC Higher Education Report No. 2. The George Washington University, School of Education and Human Development, 1991.

Homer-Dixon, Thomas. *The Ingenuity Gap: Can We Solve the Problems of the Future?* Vintage Canada, 2000.

Ifeanyi, K. C. "Minorities in Business: Black Women Make Great Leaders." *Inc.*, 22 Feb. 2012, http://www.inc.com/kc-ifeanyi/report-Black-women-make -great-leaders.html.

Johnson, Cynthia W., et al. "Bridging the Gap: 16 Years of Academic Leadership Development for Women." *NASPA Journal About Women in Higher Education*, vol. 3, no. 1, 2010, pp. 166–84, https://doi.org/10.2202/1940-7890.1049.

Kezar, Adrianna. "Leadership in Higher Education, Concepts and Theories." *Encyclopedia of International Higher Education*, edited by Jung Cheol Shin and Pedro Nuno Teixeira, editors, Springer, 2014, https://doi.org/10.1007 /978-94-017-9553-1_537-1.

King, J. E., and G. Gomez. *On the Pathway to the Presidency: Characteristics of Higher Education's Senior Leadership.* American Council on Education, 2008.

Lawrence, Keith, and Terry Keleher. "Structural Racism." *Race and Public Policy Conference Proceedings*, Boalt School of Law, University of California at Berkeley, 2004, https://www.raceforward.org/sites/default/files/pdf /188pdf.pdf.

Leal, Disney R. "The Colonizing Condition of Neoliberalism in Higher Education: What It Is, Why It Matters, and What We Can Do." *ASHE Grads*, 31 May 2019, https://ashegrads.wordpress.com/2019/05/31/the-colonizing

-condition-of-neoliberalism-in-higher-education-what-it-is-why-it-matters
-and-what-we-can-do/.

Leggett-Robinson, Pamela M., et al. "Board #87: Native-Born and Foreign-Born Black Students in STEM: Addressing STEM Identity and Belonging Barriers and their Effects on STEM Retention and Persistence at the Two Year College." *ASEE Annual Conference & Exposition Conference Proceedings*, Columbus, Ohio, 26 June 2017, https://doi.org/10.18360/1-2--27945.

Lemelle, Anthony, et al. *Dilemmas of Black Faculty at Predominantly White Institutions in the United States: Issues in the Post-multicultural Era*. Edwin Mellen Press, 2010.

Liggins-Moore, Lysa. *Forty-Three African American Women Executives' Perceptions of Challenges and Required Capabilities to Become a Leader*. 2016. Pepperdine U, PhD dissertation. *Digital Commons*, https://digitalcommons.pepperdine.edu/etd/736.

Litz, David, and Rida Blaik-Hourani. "Transformational Leadership and Change in Education." *Oxford Research Encyclopedia of Education*, edited by Rosemary Papa, Oxford UP, 2020, https://doi.org/10.1093/acrefore/9780190264093.013.631.

Madsen, Susan R. *Why Do We Need More Women Leaders in Utah?* Research & Policy Brief, no. 10, 12 Jan. 2015, https://www.usu.edu/uwlp/files/briefs/10-why-do-we-need-more-women-leaders.pdf.

———. "Women and Leadership in Higher Education: Current Realities, Challenges, and Future Directions." *Advances in Developing Human Resources*, vol. 14, no. 2, May 2012, pp. 131–39, https://doi.org/10.1177/1523422311436299.

Mainah, Fredah, and Vernita Perkins. "Challenges Facing Female Leaders of Color in U.S. Higher Education." *International Journal of African Development*, vol. 2, no. 2, 2015, pp. 5–13.

McIntosh, Peggy. "Reflections and Future Directions for Privilege Studies." *Journal of Social Issues*, vol. 68, no. 1, 2012, pp. 194–206.

Merchant, Karima. *How Men and Women Differ: Gender Differences in Communication Styles, Influence Tactics, and Leadership Styles*. 2012. Claremont U, CMC senior thesis, https://scholarship.claremont.edu/cmc_theses/513.

Montez, Joni. "Developing an Instrument to Assess Higher Education Leadership." *Annual Meeting of the American Educational Research Association*, Chicago, Illinois, 21–25 Apr. 2003, pp. 2–20, https://files.eric.ed.gov/fulltext /ED477446.pdf.

Morreale, Sherwyn P., and Constance M. Staley. "FORUM: Instructional Communication and Millennial Students: Millennials, Teaching and Learning, and the Elephant in the College Classroom." *Communication Education*, vol. 65, no. 3, 2016, pp. 370–73.

Osborn, Richard N., et al. "Toward a Contextual Theory of Leadership." *The Leadership Quarterly*, vol. 13, no. 6, 2022, pp. 797–837.

Page, Scott E. *The Difference: How the Power of Diversity Creates Better Groups, Firms, Schools, and Societies*. Princeton UP, 2007.

Parker, Patsy. "The Historical Role of Women in Higher Education." *Administrative Issues Journal Education Practice and Research*, vol. 5, no. 1, 2015, pp. 3–14, https://doi.org/10.5929/2015.5.1.1.

Parry, Ken W. "Grounded Theory and Social Process: A New Direction for Leadership Research." *The Leadership Quarterly*, vol. 9, no. 1, 1998, pp. 85–105.

Patton, D. L. "My Sister's Keeper: A Qualitative Analysis of Mentoring Experiences Among African American Women in Graduate and Professional Schools." *Journal of Higher Education*, vol. 80, no. 5, 2009, pp. 510–37.

Pierre, Fredna. *Breaking the Concrete Wall: The Challenges Facing African-American Women in the Workplace*. 2019. Salem State U, Honors thesis. *Digital Commons*, https://digitalcommons.salemstate.edu/honors_theses/237.

Poon, OiYan A. "Ending White Innocence in Student Affairs and Higher Education." *Journal of Student Affairs*, vol. 27, 2018, pp. 13–23, https://sahe.colo state.edu/wpcontent/uploads/sites/10/2018/03/SAHE-Journal-2018.pdf#

Pucciarelli, Francesca, and Andreas Kaplan. "Competition and Strategy in Higher Education: Managing Complexity and Uncertainty." *Business Horizons*, vol. 59, no. 3, 2016, pp. 311–20, https://doi.org/10.1016/j.bushor.2016.01.003.

Ryan, Christian N. *Disruptive Leadership: A Grounded Theory Study of How Three Kentucky Women Are Leading Change*. 2016. Western Kentucky U, PhD dissertation. *Digital Commons*, http://digitalcommons.wku.edu/diss/109.

Selingo, Jeffrey J. *2026, the Decade Ahead: The Seismic Shifts Transforming the Fu-

ture of Higher Education. The Chronicle of Higher Education, 2016, https://www.yhc.edu/sites/default/files/about/depts_services/planning_assessment/The%20Chronicle%202026%20The%20decade%20ahead.pdf.

Squire, Dian, et al. "Plantation Politics and Neoliberal Racism in Higher Education: A Framework for Reconstructing Anti-Racist Institutions." *Teachers College Record*, vol. 120, 2018, p. 140307.

Stirgus, Eric. "Dearth of Diversity in Leadership at Georgia's Top Colleges." *The Atlanta Journal-Constitution*, 20 Nov. 2020, https://www.ajc.com/education/dearth-of-diversity-in-leadership-at-georgias-top-colleges/VRZJRDMJP5DQBAUWT6SEVSGUBQ/.

Thompson, Sarah A., and Karen L. Miller. "Disruptive Trends in Higher Education: Leadership Skills for Successful Leaders." *Journal of Professional Nursing*, vol. 34, 2018, pp. 92–96.

Valverde, Leonard A. *Leaders of Color in Higher Education: Unrecognized Triumphs in Harsh Institutions.* Alta Mira Press, 2003.

Wallace, Sherri L., et al. "Black Women as Scholars and Social Agents: Standing in the Gap." *The Negro Educational Review*, vol. 65, nos. 1–4, 2014, pp. 44–61.

Wallenstein, Peter, editor. *Higher Education and the Civil Rights Movement: White Supremacy, Black Southerners, and College Campuses.* UP of Florida, 2008.

West, Candace, and Don H. Zimmerman. "Doing Gender." *Gender & Society*, vol. 1, no. 2, 1987, pp. 125–51, https://doi.org/10.1177/0891243287001002002.

Wildavsky, Ben, et al. *Reinventing Higher Education: The Promise of Innovation.* Harvard Education Press, 2011.

Wilder, Craig Steven. *Ebony and Ivy: Race, Slavery, and the Troubled History of America's Universities.* Bloomsbury Press, 2013.

Williams, John L. *Desegregating America's Colleges and Universities: Title VI Regulations of Higher Education.* Teachers College Press, 1988.

Williamson, Joy Ann. *Radicalizing the Ebony Tower: Black Colleges and the Black Freedom Struggle in Mississippi.* Teachers College Press, 2008.

Wolfman, B. R. "Lights as from Beacon: African American Administrators in the Academy." *Black Women in the Academy: Promises and Perils*, edited by Lois Benjamin, UP of Florida, 1997, pp. 158–67.

Woolley, Anita W. "Evidence for a Collective Intelligence Factor in the Performance of Human Groups." *Science*, vol. 330, no. 6004, 2010 Oct. 29, pp. 686–88, https://doi.org/10.1126/science.1193147.

AFTERWORD

Strategies and Lessons for Changing the Leadership Landscape in Higher Education

MANGALA SUBRAMANIAM AND M. CRISTINA ALCALDE

T he voices of women of color and their work on diversity as leaders have rarely been discussed in scholarly work and in scholarship on the history of higher education. At the same time, recent racial justice movements and the COVID-19 pandemic have pushed institutions to recognize how racism and violence especially impact people of color, and often disproportionately Black and African American people, within and outside of our institutions of higher education. During this time, conversations about the importance of more intentionally diversifying institutions and working toward more equitable and inclusive practices have become possible in spaces in which perhaps they may not have been possible just a few years ago. Yet, cultural change is slow and structural obstacles, founded on histories of oppression and exclusion, persist in many spaces and are not transformed as quickly as we need them to change. For women of color, leadership—especially senior leadership—and demands for change continue to be difficult to navigate, even as more and more change and cultural transformation are demanded by students, faculty, and staff within.

As we have noted, there are few women of color in upper levels of university leadership, and in fact, leadership in higher education is gendered and racialized in deep-rooted ways. Embedded norms, gendered and racialized stereotypes, and suspicion of women of color leaders limit change. Even when efforts are initiated, such as by the contributors in this collection, they face personal and professional risks. The "work" of leadership, and particularly that related to diversity, equity, and inclusion that is most times shouldered by women of color at middle and lower layers of university administration, is either met with resistance or rendered invisible. Yet the African American, Asian American, and Latinx women leaders who reflect on and examine their experiences in this volume have contributed to making "scratches" on the wall (see González in this volume).

In this afterword, we bring together the chapters by focusing on some of the lessons and recommendations gleaned from contributors' experiences and strategies that may be useful for leaders and future leaders at all levels as women of color leaders navigate the higher education landscape. In doing this, we consider why such experiences, with some exceptions, are yet to be integrated theoretically and analytically into scholarship despite the many public pronouncements of "commitments" to diversity made by institutions of higher education. We foreground the need to recognize and change the deeply gendered and racialized spaces in which we lead, live, and work. Through these lessons and recommendations, we foreground three overlapping themes that are intertwined in the experiential narratives of the authors: the multiple marginalities experienced in predominantly white institutions (PWIs), the associated professional and personal costs and barriers to sustainable diversity work, and the responsibility of leaders to frame and take action to foster diversity, equity, and inclusion.

LESSONS AND RECOMMENDATIONS

The leadership pathways and practices discussed in this volume result in several concrete lessons and recommendations. We learn from the chapters in this book that as we rewrite the history of higher education to include the leadership of women of color, we must acknowledge both the successes and the accompanying heavy toll on women's personal and professional lives of these experiences. There are some structural issues we can glean from recent studies and data that unequivocally point to the underrepresentation of women, and more specifically women of color, in higher education leadership. For example, a 2021 report shows that while women make up 60% of higher ed professionals, they make up only 24% of top earners overall, and women of color, in particular, make up only 2.5% of top earners (Silbert and Mach Dubé). What it means to inhabit the spaces in which women work toward change, as leaders, and, less often, as top earners, also needs to be examined.

The first lesson, then, is that it is necessary and urgent to tell our counterstories—as Esperanza and Hodges and Welch encourage us to do—to ensure that the history of higher education includes the complicated and sometimes harrowing realities of women of color. The number of women of color in formal leadership positions remains small, yet the stories we tell—the result of our scholarly expertise and life experiences—provide significant knowledge about the issues women of color face and the many ways women of color experience leadership in higher education. Here we have focused on the counterstories of women of color in PWIs. Telling these stories is not only courageous but risky and costly. It is risky and fraught with immediate and long-term costs because we become, those of us who embody difference and are commonly marked as outsiders, knowingly or unknowingly vulnerable to suspicion of pushing too hard or too much within spaces of institutionalized white fragility. In these spaces, we may be punished for too loudly critiquing institutional practices and structures and refusing to be complicit in our own silencing. Rather than isolated stories, taken together, the counterstories of Alcalde and Henne-Ochoa, Esperanza, González, Legget-Robinson and Scott-Johnson, Subramaniam and Kokan, and Hodges and Welch loudly and collectively demand that we recognize the institutional failures across locations that result in personal and professional costs and

prevent sustainable change. These are the stories behind the low numbers of women of color in senior leadership roles. These counterstories
are testaments to the need for institutional change. By recognizing and
learning from them, we move further away from the common practice of
women of color leaders hitting up against brick walls in doing diversity
and social justice work (Ahmed) and closer to demolishing those walls.
We make visible the routine ways in which women may be or have been
thrown out of promising careers in the twists and turns of the labyrinth
of women's leadership in the academy (Eagly and Carli).

A second connected lesson is that these stories are not homogenous,
and solidarity is not equivalent to sameness. More specifically, these
stories caution us against grouping all "women and people of color" together as institutions create plans to enhance diversity, equity, and inclusion across all areas and levels of leadership. We must more deeply
look and learn. Looking and learning more deeply allows others and
ourselves to recognize differences among women of color, even as we
are grouped together as "diverse" and as we intentionally learn from and
work to support one another across our differences to build sustainable
solidarities. African American, Asian, and Latinx women may share
the experience of microaggressions and bias, yet our identities and life
and career trajectories are also embedded in distinct histories, experiences, and needs. Just as among the contributors in this volume, we hear
and learn from leaders from a variety of backgrounds—immigrant status, nationality, language, gender, racial, ethnic, and class. In part, the
institutional failures and resulting extra labor on and microaggressions
against women of color come from an overarching assumption of ho-
mogeneity and dismissal and devaluing of specific histories of lived experiences. Esperanza, of Filipino descent, for example, narrates how her
colleagues assumed that because she is brown and Asian, she knew how
to pronounce Chinese names and that those same identities made her
accessible to all students of color.

More broadly, when institutions announce recruitment or retention goals as a specific percentage or number of "diverse individuals"
or "women and people of color," the stated institutional goals of the
anti-racist statements Subramaniam and Kokan discuss may quickly
become meaningless. In their analysis of the anti-racist statements released by 130 doctoral institutions in the United States, Subramaniam
and Kokan remind us that lofty goals and statements do not necessarily
reflect who is, in practice, included and represented at each level of the
institution, nor do these reflect the understanding of differences among
groups. Henne-Ochoa discusses how within a specific group (in her case,
Latinx) differences of positionality, gender, and power also create frictions "within the family." Acknowledging these differences and tensions
is part of the process of developing and examining sustainable solidarities, transformation, and change.

The third lesson is that committees, task forces, and anti-racist statements cannot take the place of educating and capacity building. The
composition and time line for the work greatly influence what task forces
and committees can accomplish and roll into action. Sometimes committees exist for long periods of time, and they are kept busy with discussions and writing reports, and at other times, it is a desire for a quick
turnaround to be perceived as being responsive. The lack of a middle
ground in terms of time and scope can impact adversely the consideration of issues and action. Additionally, committees or task forces are
often compelled to contain the breadth and depth of the work they do
either because of the boundaries set or because the committee may be
filled with the "usual suspects." Even when it seems like faculty of color
are involved in task forces or committees and therefore involved in key
decision-making pertaining to diversity and equity, it is important to
examine who they are and to point out if they are the "usual suspects"
who are unlikely to pursue bold steps. There is a need to draw a clear
line between what it means to bring in diverse voices to a conversation

or committee versus the expectation of compliance and agreement by white and or male leaders. The inclusion of diverse voices will involve varying opinions and experiences that must be carefully weighed by leaders whose own knowledge is key to responding to those variations. Additionally, committees or task forces become spaces for exerting power across administrators and represented constituencies and may lead to a discussion of who's the more oppressed (Sue, *Overcoming Our Racism*, *Race Talk*), relying on a less-than-constructive form of diversity Olympics and bringing about little potential for transformation and solidarity-building.

As noted by Subramaniam and Kokan, there is unlikely to be an evenness in knowledge and understanding of terminology such as diversity and equity by members of committees or task forces that can curtail meaningful discussions and not recognize the commonalities and differences across underrepresented groups. These aspects call for attention to the importance and need for understanding terminology to ensure there is no soft-pedaling of needed action. Arguments for distributing "diversity work" so that women and faculty of color are not unduly burdened are complicated, and so being attentive to who can bring knowledge and expertise to bear on critical discussions is essential. Enlisting more than the "usual suspects" who are faces of color and who may or may not focus on diversity work for top leaders to "use" for their own agenda rather than for change can go a long way for transformation and to ensure that committees and task forces make bold recommendations and are held accountable.

Capacity building should occur continuously and must be required of top administrators, as well as of all key constituencies on a campus. As noted by Alcalde and Henne-Ochoa, students must be prepared to "learn about and engage with the histories and realities of oppression, exclusion, and racism in the United States and the world more broadly" (p. 121). In fact, many universities are only now beginning serious discussions about requirements of courses related to race and ethnicity. This is, as noted by Alcalde and Henne-Ochoa, critical to address the experiences of Black, Indigenous, and People of Color students whose histories and experiences are too often invisible. Alcalde worked within an academic unit to create a specific diversity requirement for undergraduate students. The course requirement on race and ethnicity became effective, after final senate approval, in the fall of 2021, after she had left the institution to pursue a new role. As noted earlier, we also need to move beyond students. Education of those who are unfamiliar with what it means to be racially and ethnically different is needed to propose changes and act upon changing the face of leadership, especially at the highest levels. These sorts of changes have been slow and directly impact and limit the pace of institutional change. Over and over again, culture change is propelled by women of color, who bear the disproportionate weight on their shoulders. This brings us to the fourth lesson we identify as important.

As women of color are continuously banging their heads against the wall in their efforts to bring about change, and while the number of scratches on the wall may continue to increase (cf. González), the wall remains. Women of color in administrative positions have to continuously be resilient and hold their heads high about the "diversity work" they do despite attempts by some to scuttle their work, pull them down, or stereotype and isolate them. Such experiences can become overbearing, especially when women of color lack role models and mentors. So when women avoid or step away from leadership positions, it is often not because they are not qualified or skilled (see Esperanza) but because of the overt and covert form of bias that beat down on them, because they go against the unwritten status quo rules. Women must, and do, make decisions to protect themselves. There is a deep need for trusted mentorship and advising to build confidence and reinforce abilities (see González). We note that mentorship is like a twin for women of color leadership.

Recognition of the work of women of color can contribute to confidence building and reassurances about our abilities and knowledge, in a positive but not patronizing way. Recognition may also be about rewards, and asks that we also consider what is left "hidden"—accomplishments or achievements that are never acknowledged, mentioned, or tangibly recognized. Women of color in leadership positions need advocates and support to be able to do diversity, equity, and inclusion work without the usual "roadblocks." As Subramaniam reflects on her position, she notes that support from allies and those in positions of authority can be instrumental, yet this sort of work still requires tremendous resilience on the part of women of color (see Subramaniam and Kokan). All contributors emphasize the personal costs—to self, to family—of their commitment to their work in the context of prevalent biases and obstacles.

To complement these four lessons, our contributors also offer recommendations. Legget-Robinson and Scott-Johnson recommend disruptive leadership as essential for change. They remind us that this requires navigating slowly but surely, and that tact and grit are key elements. Their chapter underscores disruptive leadership as a form of leadership possible only when it is possible to challenge hegemony, incorporate (not merely represent) marginal voices, and question as well as assess the root of problems. At the same time, as pointed out by Hodges and Welch, institutions should not recruit and hire agents of change and then criticize them for disrupting the status quo. How can disruptive leadership become possible? We underscore three possible ways to engage in disruptive leadership.

Hodges and Welch recommend that institutions alter the typical model of a desirable leader as one who is attractive based on, in large part, the potential for their fame or reputation to raise the institution's visibility and standing. Bringing in the words of late Congressman John Lewis, they call on leaders in higher education to also "make some noise and get in good, necessary trouble" for the cause of racial justice and equality. Instead of troublemakers, however, leaders in higher education too often fail as role models when their responses to concerns, particularly racial incidents, are simply programmed (see Subramaniam and Kokan), and they fall short of transforming structures. It is important to aim to attract and retain bold leaders who do not fit into the expected mold of white, male, compliant, and/or "rational." Internal restructuring of institutions to enable the revision or cancellation of impractical and outdated practices that hinder change should be steps taken by bold leaders.

Top-down administration that leads to hoarding of power maintains the status quo that in turn reinforces gender and racial inequities. Respecting and adopting a shared governance approach can deconcentrate power to some degree. As the experiences of all contributors in this book underscore, resistance to a revised and more equitable distribution of power (true shared governance, some might say) is at the heart of many forms of bias and exclusion experienced by women of color leaders. We need leaders who not only talk and issue statements about diversity but also walk the messy, necessary path of reenvisioning leadership, governance, and the process of change. As Alcalde and Henne-Ochoa remind us, "The disruption of hierarchical processes always has the potential to cause discomfort to those who inhabit the institution's white masculine norms and habits" (p. 109). This contrasts with the more common practice of those who inhabit more marginalized spaces being expected to suppress or make invisible their own discomfort to ensure the comfort of those around them, which then tends to sustain rather than change dominant structures.

As we seek to change institutions and recognize the importance of diversity and change in leadership, a second connected recommendation is to more intentionally consider and evaluate how inserting the term *diversity* in a position title on the one hand and being perceived as embodying diversity, on the other hand, may impact the leadership trajectory of an individual, and more generally, the potential for change for an institution. Alcalde and Henne-Ochoa caution us against an "add diversity and stir" approach that fails to create meaningful, sustainable change.

Johnson and Hekman found that among top executives in the business world, people of color, and women more broadly, who promoted diversity were penalized by being perceived as less competent and effective leaders than white leaders. In contrast, they found that the in-group bias of white leaders that led to the reproduction of whiteness at the top was not scrutinized and, in fact, tended to be rewarded. In higher education, the chapters in this book similarly point to how the competence of women of color is consistently challenged and their focus on diversity penalized. Often, as in the case of assumptions made about Esperanza, their embodiment of difference is interpreted as an invitation to assign more invisible labor, while their leadership trajectory beyond the realm of "diversity" is denied. As Alcalde and Henne-Ochoa suggest, the increasing demand for chief diversity officers and for unit-based diversity officers does not necessarily translate into power for the individuals in those positions. Moving forward, it will be important for those in leadership positions focused on diversity and those around them to more carefully evaluate how a position focused on diversity is or is not attached to an institution's economic and political resources and how such focus may impact the leadership trajectories of the women of color tapped for those positions.

The third recommendation is for white leaders to more carefully listen to the voices and experiences of women of color and incorporate them into actions, even when they see and hear what is different than the typical white and/or male experiences, and not be dismissive or explain it away. For instance, Hodges and Welch emphasize the importance of initiating action for racial equity from the top. University leaders at the top must "engage with leaders of color and skillful diversity practitioners in honest conversations and welcome these partners to participate in framing a new structure and way of operating" (p. 73). Ensuring representation and inclusion of partners from across racial and ethnic groups is critical for broad-based change and to avoid setting up competing interests across the groups. As pointed out by Hodges and Welch, leaders must acknowledge their own responsibility in sustaining inequities and commit to action to move forward. While this may not be easy for individual leaders, it must be pursued, "particularly when the initiatives they develop can serve as models of, and even the motivation for, substantive change" (p. 73).

Esperanza explains how lack of support adversely affected her leadership possibilities and trajectory. First budget cuts led to restructuring of the campus initiatives she was handling, then to a change in top leadership. A cascade of changes in the initiatives followed, and, without input or consultation, Esperanza was sidelined with responsibility for summer orientation programs. Despite the new provost's assurance of the relevance of her diminished responsibility being explained as recognition for her "aptitude for community building," she was being pulled into doing more social and emotional labor and shut out from taking on a greater leadership role. Such experiences raise two points pertinent for leaders. First, institutions must recognize and reward the emotional labor that women of color, especially as leaders, do. This labor is not tangibly measurable, yet it is central to diversity work. Perhaps these aspects play into the pay and power gap reported by Silbert and Mach Dubé. Second, the lack of transparency in how initiatives are created and disbanded speaks to the lack of consistency in the goals of leaders and the lack of inclusion of input from women of color leaders.

Listening to the voices of women of color requires leaders to understand commonalities of experiences as well as differences among them and avoid relying on the "usual suspects" who fail to be critical of the lack of action for diversity and equity. Leaders must be cognizant that surveys about climate and collegiality fail to capture the voices of women of color when they are isolated in units and which is not very different across layers of leadership (Alcalde and Subramaniam). This brings us back to the urgent need for diversifying leadership by making space for racial and ethnic minorities to thrive in, and be compensated for, doing diversity and equity work.

CONCLUDING THOUGHTS: MULTIPLE MARGINALITIES, NEW FORMS OF LEADERSHIP

All the contributors in this volume narrate experiences fueled by a desire for change and for action for the transformation of institutions, even as they recognize the marginality of their positions. The authors may be space invaders in a leadership terrain that is far from conducive to women of color joining. In this section, we return to the question we started with: What does it mean to embody change as a leader of color in a space of normative masculinity and whiteness? Across differences in professional and personal backgrounds, disciplines, administrative roles, the experiences of the women of color in this book foreground that leadership is always already gendered and racialized and that disrupting long-standing structures and hierarchies carries professional and personal costs. As discussed in the chapters, the authors, in different leadership positions, navigate the terrain by serving as informal or disruptive leaders and strategically weighing the risks associated with their diversity and equity work.

Contending with institutional structures or banging our heads against the wall, to use Ahmed's metaphor, has made women of color leaders more resilient by strategically deploying silence. Silence may be the appropriate or deliberate strategy when women of color leaders are asked about the challenges they face. Disruptive leaders are not creating waves of change overnight but pushing for equity knowing that they may be excluded or silenced along the way and as a result of these lengthy efforts. They may also choose to be silent. That is, silence may be a means of resistance or a political tool to express dissent in an institutional system within which women of color leaders are compelled to provide proof of their own and others' experiences of racism, exclusion, and devaluation. Women of color leaders are expected to contribute to diversity but rarely have the power to affect the change toward sustainable diversity and equity.

The knowledge constructed in this volume by marginalized leaders is based on experiences and administrative and academic expertise, and our aim has been to bring these multilayered, collective experiences to the center as resources to transform institutions that have predominantly white and/or male leadership. The experiential narratives we include provide a glimpse into the immense work of women of color who are engaged in disrupting the white spaces of higher education. We encourage leaders and future leaders to follow the few who have worked to create pathways and to more intentionally widen these pathways through institutional resources and changes. Institutions of higher education are responsible for increasing and widening the pathways for women of color leaders. This work, we have individually and collectively asserted, cannot be placed on a single individual or small set of individuals who either embody or have "diversity" in their position titles. Institutions must confront their own biases in who gets appointed to leadership roles and in the parameters of those leadership roles. This is urgently needed in considering how skills, "collegiality," "fit," and temperament are embedded in cultures of whiteness. In practice, even the very concept of leadership has long been associated with white, elite masculinity and continues to elevate individualism, competition, and aggression over inclusion and relationality (Liu). This means that efforts to create more inclusive forms of leadership by women of color deans, associate, and assistant deans, advising leaders, and others that appear in this volume are met with suspicion at best and, most often, by strong overt and covert forms of resistance in response both to the positioning and the practices of these leaders. In this context, talk of diversifying administration and leadership by recruiting and retaining "women and people of color" may be shorthand for white women, who have made more gains than women of color and who far outpace the representation of women of color in faculty and administrative positions.

The role of innovative and diverse leaders is further reinforced in the current context of the pandemic and the protests for racial justice, which have affected people's daily lives in profound ways. These effects will continue to have long-term impacts within academia. The inequities that exist in "normal" times do not disappear during a pandemic; rather, they are exacerbated. Women of color face higher burdens, and vulnerable faculty are also likely to be uncomfortable articulating COVID-19 impacts. Institutional leaders are therefore responsible for ensuring who is represented at the table, whose voices are heard, who is asked to lead and given the resources to enact change, and which voices are incorporated in recommendations and actions.

So what new forms of institutional leadership will allow for transformation? The disruptive leadership contributors collectively develop through their experiences and expertise is one that is diverse, transparent, and willing to engage in shared governance (in the true sense). It is leadership that values making bold decisions that incorporate the voices of marginal and minoritized groups and not the "usual suspects." Such leadership must combine knowledge and expertise with experiential knowledge, not hunches or good intentions, to make decisions. Short and long-term strategic visioning that is multilayered, transparent, and accountable can be impactful for sustainable change on an even keel and not in fits and starts. These transformative and inclusive forms of leadership are not new. The women of color in these pages, and many others across institutions, embody and enact these forms of leadership. It is time to recognize their counterstories and leadership; value, support, and reward their expertise, experience, and contributions; and increase institutional accountability in asking and exploring what else is needed to finally bring down the walls women of color leaders have now made unstable. Ensuring that women of color leaders have the power and authority to excel is critical for change within institutions.

WORKS CITED

Ahmed, Sara. *On Being Included: Racism and Diversity in Institutional Life*. Duke UP, 2012.

Alcalde, Cristina M., and Mangala Subramaniam. "Women in Leadership Positions: Challenges and Recommendations." *Inside Higher Ed*, 17 July 2020, https://www.insidehighered.com/views/2020/07/17/women-leadership -academe-still-face-challenges-structures-systems-and-mind-sets.

Eagly, Alice, and Linda L. Carli. *Leadership for the Common Good Through the Labyrinth: The Truth About How Women Become Leaders*. Harvard Business School Press, 2007.

Johnson, Stephanie K., and David R. Hekman. "Women and Minorities Are Penalized for Promoting Diversity." *Harvard Business Review*, 23 Mar. 2016, https://hbr.org/2016/03/women-and-minorities-are-penalized-for -promoting-diversity.

Liu, Helena. "Just the Servant: An Intersectional Critique of Servant Leadership." *Journal of Business Ethics*, vol. 156, 2019, pp. 1099–112.

Silbert, Andrea, and Christy Mach Dubé. *The Power Gap Among Top Earners at America's Elite Universities*. Eos Foundation, 2021.

Sue, Derald W. *Overcoming Our Racism: The Journey to Liberation*. Jossey-Bass, 2003.

———. *Race Talk and the Conspiracy of Silence: Understanding and Facilitating Difficult Dialogues*. John Wiley & Sons, 2015.

CONTRIBUTORS

M. CRISTINA ALCALDE is vice president of Institutional Diversity and Inclusion and professor of global and intercultural studies at Miami University. From 2007 to 2021, she she served as associate dean of inclusion and internationalization in the College of Arts and Sciences and as professor of gender and women's studies and the Marie Rich Endowed Professor at the University of Kentucky. Her books include *Peruvian Lives Across Borders: Power, Exclusion, and Home* (2018); *The Woman in the Violence: Gender, Poverty, and Resistance in Peru* (2010); *La mujer en la violencia* (Spanish edition, 2014); and the coedited volumes *#MeToo and Beyond: Perspectives on a Global Movement* (with Paula-Irene Villa, 2022) and *Provocations: A Transnational Reader in the History of Feminist Thought* (with Susan Bordo and Ellen Rosenman, 2015). She has also published widely in journals and edited collections and speaks nationally and internationally on her research areas of inclusion, gender violence, migration, exclusion, belonging, leadership, and race and racialization. She has written shorter pieces for *Inside Higher Ed* on the experiences of women in leadership positions (coauthored with Subramaniam, July 2020) and on the need to reenvision leadership in higher education to be more inclusive of women of color (December 2021), as well as for *Ms.* magazine on burnout among women of color (October 2021).

JENNIFER SANTOS ESPERANZA served as professor and departmental cochair of anthropology at Beloit College, where she taught from 2008 to 2021. She received her BA in Linguistics and Cultural Anthropology from the University of Southern California, and her MA and PhD from the University of California, Los Angeles. Dr. Esperanza has conducted research on the political economy of ethnic art, which has been published in various journals, such as *Research in Economic Anthropology* and *Material Culture Review*. She has presented and published papers on decolonizing anthropology and storytelling as a pedagogical and advising strategy. She has performed for storytelling outlets such as *The Moth, Love Wisconsin*, and *80 Minutes Around the World: Stories of Immigration*. After her promotion to full professorship, she decided to leave academia. She now serves as director of diversity, equity, and inclusion for Coopera Consulting, a consulting firm that improves financial inclusion for underbanked and historically underserved populations.

TANYA GONZÁLEZ is a professor in the English department at Kansas State University and currently serves as interim associate provost for institutional effectiveness, with responsibilities in faculty and academic affairs. González served as the 2019–20 faculty senate president and continues to work on faculty success and university policy issues related to diversity, equity, and inclusion in her current position. Her research interests include Latinx literature and the Gothic, immigration in American literature, Latinx representations in popular culture, and higher education leadership. In addition to publishing in a variety of peer-reviewed journals, she is the coauthor, with Eliza Rodriguez y Gibson, of *Humor and Latina/o Camp in Ugly Betty* (Lexington, 2015).

CARMEN HENNE-OCHOA, PhD, serves as assistant dean for diversity and inclusion in the College of Arts and Sciences at Indiana University Bloomington. She earned her master's and PhD from the University of Chicago. As a sociologist, her research and teaching have focused on questions of social stratification and identity formation processes. At the core of her work and practice is interrogating disparities in the context of embodied difference and their connection to larger systems of privilege, power, and oppression. In her administrative role, she partners with divisional deans, department chairs, faculty, and staff to envision, develop, and implement strategic and foundational efforts that support the ongoing positive transformation of the College's DEIJ (diversity, equity, inclusion, and justice) culture and climate.

CAROLYN R. HODGES is professor of German emerita and vice provost and dean emerita, Graduate School, University of Tennessee, Knoxville. Her research focus has been on Black German literature and culture, multicultural education, and educational leadership. She currently serves on the executive board of the Georgiana Simpson Society for German Diaspora Studies. Her most recent book, coauthored with Olga M. Welch, is *Truth Without Tears: African American Women Deans Share Lessons in Leadership* (Harvard Education Press, 2018). Hodges earned MA and PhD degrees in German studies at the University of Chicago and a BA degree in French at Arcadia University, Pennsylvania.

ZEBA KOKAN serves as a health policy research fellow at the Weitzman Institute. Previously, she was a research assistant at the Susan Bulkeley Butler Center for Leadership Excellence and special assistant at the Consumer Financial Protection Bureau's Office of Minority and Women Inclusion. Kokan earned her bachelor's degree in brain and behavioral sciences and global studies from Purdue University. Her undergraduate senior thesis examined the politicization of trauma and identity and its role in undermining the mental health of marginalized groups. She hopes to link the social body to the human body by using interdisciplinary methods informed by people's voices and stories. Kokan was named a 2020 Truman Scholar and a 2020 Rhodes Scholarship finalist. She takes great inspiration from her paternal grandmother, Dr. Iqbalunnisa Kokan, the first Muslim woman in India to receive a PhD in mathematics, and her maternal grandmother, Sadiqa Begum, whose fiery commitment to her daughter's right to an education paved the way for generations.

PAMELA M. LEGGETT-ROBINSON, PhD, CAPM, founder and executive director of PLR Consulting in Atlanta, Georgia, has fifteen-plus years of higher education experience, which includes science, technology, engineering, and mathematics (STEM) academic leadership, STEM coaching, data analytics, academic and student success programming, and program evaluation. She holds a PhD in physical organic chemistry from Georgia State University and is a certified associate of project management. PLR Consulting works with organizations and institutions to develop and optimize STEM programs through management and evaluation. Dr. Leggett-Robinson creates successful STEM ecosystems for marginalized groups, especially women of color, by way of PLR Consulting, authorship, workshops, and speaking engagements.

PAMELA E. SCOTT-JOHNSON, PhD, currently serves as the provost and senior vice president of academic affairs at Monmouth University in West Long Branch, New Jersey. She previously served as the dean of the College of Natural and Social Sciences at California State University, Los Angeles. She earned a BA in psychology from Spelman College and an MA and PhD in psychology and neuroscience from Princeton University. Her research interests include chemosensory sciences and the psychosocial factors impacting women in the academy. As an administrator, she focuses on ensuring quality education and access for all students, identifying and developing leadership talent among faculty, creating a diverse and inclusive environment to meet the institutional mission and priorities, and increasing institutional capacity.

MANGALA SUBRAMANIAM is professor of sociology and Butler Chair and Director of the Susan Bulkeley Butler Center for Leadership Excellence at Purdue University. In her current administrative role, she focuses on providing opportunities to enhance leadership skills and professional development for faculty. The key initiatives she has created for faculty success includes the Coaching and Resource Network for assistant and associate professors (see www.purdue.edu/butler). Her keen ability to be inclusive of various constituencies on campus has led to the great success of the center's initiatives. Her coauthored piece (with Alcalde) in *Inside Higher Ed* (July 2020) provides recommendations for advancing women to leadership positions. This is reflective of her expanded research interests in the areas of gender and leadership, careers in the academy, and inclusive excellence. Her work has been highlighted in various higher education sources, such as *Chronicle of Higher Education*, *Inside Higher Ed*, and *Higher Education Digest*. She is the current state codirector of the American Council on Education Women's Network of Indiana. Subramaniam has held elected offices as treasurer of the Sociologists for Women in Society and secretary/treasurer and council member of the Sex and Gender Section of the American Sociological Association. She has also served as a member of the editorial board of *Gender and Society*, the premier scholarly sociological journal for gender-related research and was an associate editor of *Social Problems*, one of the top four journals in sociology.

OLGA M. WELCH is professor of instructional leadership emerita and dean emerita, School of Education, Duquesne University. Her research focus is educational leadership in secondary schools and higher education. She currently serves on the editorial board of the *Journal of Negro Education*. Her most recent book, coauthored with Carolyn R. Hodges, is *Truth Without Tears: African American Women Deans Share Lessons in Leadership* (Harvard Education Press, 2018). Welch earned an MS in education of the deaf and hard of hearing and an EdD in educational leadership at the University of Tennessee, Knoxville. She has a BA in history from Howard University.

INDEX

Page numbers in italics refer to figures and tables

A

ACE. *See* American Council of Education

active listening, 106

advisement in SLACs: conflict-resolution and, 87; culturally relevant pedagogy for, 87–90; debunking myths about, 95–96; derailment of, 90–93; faculty of color providing, 80, 84–85; good advisement, 85; as high-impact practice, 79–81; inequity in, 82–86; little preparation, 84–85; for marginalized students, 80; as monitoring and mentoring, 81–82; monitoring of, 86; next steps for, 95–96; open-ended questions for, 86; persistence and belonging issues, 82; recruiting for, 92; redefining and decolonizing of, 86–87; seminars for, 88–89; stereotyping in, 84; storytelling in, 87–88; student retention and, 84–85; surveys for, 85–86; training strategy for, 90; unnatural terrain for, 81–82

affinity space, 116–18

African Americans, 31, 36; African American studies, 125; college presidents, 172; COVID-19 pandemic impacting, 70; distinct history, experience, and needs, 190; HBCUs and, 160; racism and violence impacting, 187; scrutiny of, 12; university leadership, 188. *See also* Black women; faculty of color; students of color; women of color

agreement, 192

Ahmed, Sara, 2, 5, 13, 154, 198; on diversity, 58, 124, 132–33; on guests in PWIs, 62–63; on insistence, 144; on institutional immobility, 140; on institutional structures, 133; misfits coined by, 136; on policies, 147; on queer use, 136–37, 149–51; on responsibility for whiteness, 65; on restrictions and blockages, 151; on scratched walls, 135, 137–38; on wench in the works, 147–48

Alcalde, Cristina M, 7–9, 101–02, 104–06, 113–15, 121–25; counterstory, 189; on demand for diversity officers, 196; on disruption of hierarchical processes, 195; on student learning, 192–93

alliances: ethnicity and, 30; racism study addressing, 30–33, 32, 37–38. *See also* solidarity

alternate identity stories, 143

American Council of Education (ACE), 169

Angelou, Maya, 71
antebellum life, 68
anti-immigrant attacks, 142
anti-racism, 1, 10, 59, 121–22, 191; racism study addressing, 29, 31; training, 146
anxiety, 80
Anzaldúa, Gloria, 131–32, 143, 153–54
APLU. *See* Association for Public and Land Grant Universities
appropriation of women's work, 107–13, 119–20
Asian Americans, 31, 36; COVID-19 and, 22–23; distinct history, experience, and needs, 190; as model minority, 83; university leadership, 188
Association for Public and Land Grant Universities (APLU), 145, 148
Atlanta Journal-Constitution, 173, 174
Auburn University, 34
authentic leadership, 143

B

Banaji, Mahzarin R., 1–2
behavioral theories of leadership, 162
Bell, Derrick, 56, 64
Beloit College, 81, 87–90
belonging, 69, 137, 141, 153; as advisement issue, 82
Bensimon, Estela M., 162
bias, 3; gender bias, 117, 165, 178; microaggressions and, 64; overt and covert, 193; racism study addressing, 30
binary thinking, 22–23
Black, Indigenous, and People of Color (BIPOC), 132, 153, 193
Black Lives Matter (BLM), 22, 29, 121
Black women: academics, 40, 63;

college presidents, 169–70, 170, 172; as college presidents, 170; concrete ceiling and, 167; constructivist approach for, 177; disruptive leadership and, 165; as disruptive leaders in higher education, 176–78; exclusion and, 167; glass ceiling and, 167; leadership and, 12–14, 58, 157–58, 165–67; leadership at HBCUs, 168–69; as outsider-within, 67; as role models, 179; self-development, 179; stereotypes shattered by, 169; strategies for disruptive leadership, 175–76; students, 160; tenure for, 168–69. *See also* women of color
Blindspot (Banaji and Greenwald), 1–2
BLM. *See* Black Lives Matter
Bolman, Lee G., 2
Bonner, Florence, 168–69
Boston College, 34
Boston University, 34
Brandeis University, 35
bropropriators, 107
Brown University, 34
Brown v. the Board of Education, 57
Buller, Jeffrey L., 2
burnout, 80, 136

C

cakewalk, 68–69
capacity-building, 41
Carnegie Mellon University, 35
Case Western Reserve University, 28
CDOs. *See* chief diversity officers
celebrity, culture of, 68
Change Leadership in Higher Education (Buller), 2
chief diversity officers (CDOs): in PWIs, 99–100; role of, 125; skills for, 104; women of color as, 100

Christensen, Clayton M., 164
Chun, Edna, 2
City University of New York, 34
class, 6, 19, 23, 190; exclusion and, 158; ideals, 85
Clinton, William, 71
Cole, Eddie R., 19–20, 30, 38
Collaborative on Academic Careers in Higher Education, 152
College and University Professional Association for Human Resources, 57
college presidents, 169–70, 170, 171, 172
Collins, Patricia Hill, 67
Colorado State University, 29
color line, 59
Columbia University, 34
comfort work, 110
commitment, 21, 31, 35, 178; to diversity, 126, 188; to social justice, 59
community building, 106
compliance, 71, 100, 192
concrete ceiling, 167
confidence-building, 194
conflict-resolution, 87
connective awareness, 177
constructivist approach, 177
contingency theories of leadership, 163
co-optation, 72
Cornell University, 28
counterstorytelling, 93–95; of Alcalde, 189; caution from, 190; of Henne-Ochoa, 189; urgency for, 189–90; by women of color, 200
covert bias, 193
COVID-19 pandemic, 121, 187, 200; African Americans impacted by, 70; Asian Americans and, 22–23; higher education and, 18; impact on faculty leadership social justice,

144–46; impact statements, 145, 154n4; institutional whiteness exposed by, 99; in racism study, 32; service fatigue, 148
critical race theory, 93–95
Cuba, Lee, 84
cultural change, 80, 82, 187; creation of, 95–96; push for, 125; time for, 106; women of color propelling, 193
culturally relevant pedagogy, 87–90
culture of celebrity, 68
culture-shifting work, 112

D
DACA. *See* Deferred Action for Childhood Arrivals
dating violence, 146
deaning while Black, 7; barriers and resistance to, 58–59, 61–63; challenge to status quo, 73; dismantling institutional whiteness, 70–75; diversity discussions and, 61–62; ethnicity discussions absent in, 62; gatekeeping and, 60–61; as outsider-within, 67–70; perceived as problem, 59–63; in PWIs, 55; responding to racism, 72; social justice and, 59, 69, 74; unveiling lie of whiteness, 63–67; whiteness in higher education and, 56–59; by women of color, 58
decision-making: change from, 3; by faculty of color, 191; in leadership, 200; by white men, 5; by women of color, 193
decolonized pedagogy, 86, 89, 93
Decolonizing Pedagogies Project (DPP), 87
Deferred Action for Childhood Arrivals (DACA), 141

DEI. *See* diversity, equity, and inclusion

Delgado, Denise A., 3–4

DiAngelo, Robin, 1, 64–65

Diaz, Gloria, 149

differentiated learning platforms, 175

discrimination, 32, 146, 178

disruption: disruptive wonder, 178; of exclusion, 114; of hierarchical processes, 195; in institutionalizing diversity, 104–06, 112, 116; theory of disruptive innovation, 164; of whiteness, 121–25

disruptive leadership, 14, 198; Black women and, 165; contradictory tactics in, 176; critical lens for, 158; defined, 164–65; emergent operating system for, 164; engaging in, 194–95; ingenuity gap and, 175; intersectionality and, 158, 178, 179; need for, 158–59, 175–76; need in higher education, 170, 172–73, 175; practice of, 178–79; research in, 178–79; skills for, 177; strategies, for Black women, 175–76; transformational leadership compared to, 177

diversity, 12; Ahmed on, 58, 124, 132–33; commitment to, 126, 188; demand for officers, 196; discussions, deaning while Black, 61–62; diversity in action, 60; diversity work, 13, 15, 192, 193, 194; as happy talk, 37; higher education approaches to, 5; in leadership, 9; mainstreaming of, 40; meaning to university leaders, 21–22; in paper trails, 21, 37; in position titles, 195, 199; racism study addressing, 30, 33–36, 34; statements, 64; terminology curtailing,

192; university leaders deconstructing, 74–75

diversity, equity, and inclusion (DEI), 99, 104, 125; as growing field, 101; Latinx in, 119; planning groups, 113; priorities for, 108; racism study addressing, 30, 33–36, 34; work in, 41, 114, 119

diversity, institutionalizing: curriculum for, 121–25; disruption in, 104–06, 112, 116; emotional labor in, 104–06, 112; within familial spaces, 116–21; intentionality, 104–06; men's appropriation of women's work, 107–13; microlevel process in, 106, 111, 126–27; opening and closing doors in, 103; overview, 99–103; at systemic and unit levels, 125–27; visibility in, 113–16

domestic violence, 146

double-consciousness, 59

DPP. *See* Decolonizing Pedagogies Project

Drylongso (Gwaltney), 65–66

Du Bois, W. E. B., 59–60, 69

Duke University, 31

dysfunctionality, 175, 179

E

Einstein, Alfred, 173

Emory University, 34

emotional labor: in institutionalizing diversity, 104–06, 112; as job expectation, 104

emotional openness, 106

equality, 55; good necessary trouble for, 75; racism study addressing, 33–36, 34

equity, 12, 15; defining, 39–40; as inclusion, 40; opportunity, 179; racism study addressing, 33–36, 34; terminology curtailing, 192. *See also* diversity, equity, and inclusion; inequity

Esperanza, Jennifer Santos, 6, 8, 9, 189, 190, 197

ethnicity, 24, 25, 169, 190; absent, in deaning while black, 62; alliances and, 30; college presidents by, 171; course requirements for, 121–25, 193; ethnic studies, 138; inequality and, 18

ethnocentrism, 11, 140; higher education and, 18

Evans, Alvin, 2

exclusion, 64; anger of, 72; Black exclusion, 69, 124; Black women and, 167; class and, 158; disruption of, 114; in higher education, 99, 158, 167; history of, 121, 187, 192; invisibility of, 113, 115–16; in PWIs, 158; racialized exclusion, 20–21; shared governance and, 195; women of color and, 199; worldwide, 192

F

faculty leadership, social justice and: action plan committees for, 146–47; COVID-19 pandemic and, 144–46; measurement of programs, 151–52; misfits methods in, 134–38, 140–47; overview of challenges, 131–34; policies in, 147–49; queer use in, 134–37, 147–51; scratched walls in, 134–39; steps for increased dialogue and action, 140–41; tenure elimination and, 152–53; town hall meetings for, 146

faculty of color: decision-making by, 191; inequities for, 80; in marginal spaces, 22; as mentors, 8; professorships and, 159–60; providing advisement in SLACs, 80, 84–85; in PWIs, 56–57; recruitment of, 63; retention of, 39; teacher burnout and, 80; tenure for, 85

familial spaces, 116–21

Feagin, Joe, 2

Floyd, George, 7, 11; call for protest over death, 17–18; civil unrest sparked by murder, 99; higher education and, 18; racism study addressing, 23, 29, 36

Freije, Margaret, 81

Fries-Britt, Sharon, 38

Fujiwara, Lynn, 105

G

Gallos, Joan V., 2

gatekeeping, 60–61

gender, 190, 191; gender bias, 117, 165, 178; gendered stereotypes, 187–88; gender pay, 179; LGBTQ, 139

Georgia Institute of Technology, 32–33, 35

glass ceiling, 58, 167

Glaude, Eddie, Jr., 64

Gonzalez, Carmen G., 93

González, Tanya, 10, 189

grassroots leaders, 139

Greenwald, Anthony G., 1–2

Guenter, Melissa, 20–21

Gutiérrez y Muhs, Gabriella, 2–3, 93

Gwaltney, John Langston, 65–66

H

Hansberry, Lorraine, 71

harassment, 32, 146, 147

Harper, Shaun R., 30

Harris, Angela P., 93

Harvard University, 34

HBCUs. *See* Historically Black Colleges and Universities

health care inequity, 153

hegemony, 14; challenge to, 178, 194; hegemonic masculinity, 120–21, 166; white hegemony, 103, 168

Hekman, David R., 196

Henne-Ochoa, Carmen, 7–8, 101–02, 107–12, 116–20; counterstory, 189; on demand for diversity officers, 196; on disruption of hierarchical processes, 195; on frictions within family, 191; on student learning, 192–93

Hensel, Nancy, 159–60

hepeaters, 107

Hernandez, Kathy-Ann C., 142–43

hierarchical organizations, 11, 108–10

higher education: academic ranks (2020), 161; approaches to diversity, 5; Black women as college presidents, 169–70, 170; Black women as disruptive leaders, 176–78; COVID-19 and, 18; current exclusion in, 158; devaluation of liberal arts, 173; dysfunctionality in, 179; ethnocentrism and, 18; exclusion in, 99, 158, 167; Floyd death and, 18; funding for, 173; goal of, 170–71; hierarchies, 11; history of, 158–60; history of Black women in, 160; homophobia and, 18; innovations in, 175; institutional whiteness in, 56–59; leadership in, 162–65; microaggressions in, 178; minorities in, 5; need for disruptive leadership, 170, 172–73, 175; patriarchy in, 166; plantation politics in, 159; racism and, 18; scratched walls of, 13–14; social justice and, 173; student

demographics and, 173, 174; white spaces of, 199; white world in, 1; women of color in, 5–6. *See also* university leadership

himitators, 107

Historically Black Colleges and Universities (HBCUs): African Americans and, 160; Black women leadership at, 168–69; as male-dominated, 168; tenure at, 169

Hochschild, Arlie, 120

Hodges, Carolyn R., 3, 7, 8, 9–10, 189; on hiring agents of change, 194; on top university leaders, 196–97

Homer-Dixon, Thomas, 175

homophobia, 11; higher education and, 18

hooks, bell, 68, 69

How to Be an Antiracist (Kendi), 1

Huynh, Steffi, 22, 31

hypervisibility, 112; negotiation of, 126; paradox of, 116–21; token status of, 116–17

I

inclusion, 12, 15; equity as, 40; inclusivity in pedagogy, 175; racism study addressing, 33–36, 34; university leaders deconstructing, 74–75; university leaders on, 40–41. *See also* diversity, equity, and inclusion

An Inclusive Academy (Stewart, A., and Valian), 2, 141

inequity: in advisement, 82–86; ethnicity and, 18; for faculty of color, 80; in health care, 153

ingenuity gap, 175

innovations: in higher education, 175; theory of disruptive innovation, 164

insistence, 14, 144
institutional change, 14
institutional gaslighting, 62
institutional immobility, 140
institutionalized racism, 81, 175
institutional memory, 137, 139
institutional whiteness, 1, 67, 81; approach in academia, 5–6; counter-storytelling and, 94; COVID-19 pandemic exposing, 99; deaning while Black and, 56–59; dismantling, in deaning while Black, 70–75; experience of dismantling, 9–10; studies, 24; systemic racism veiled by, 58
integrity, 178
intentionality: in institutionalizing diversity, 104–06; in transformational leadership, 177
intersectionality, 7, 26, 136; disruptive leadership and, 158, 178, 179; learned behavior and, 177; lived experience of, 178; role of, 166; transformational leadership and, 179
invisibility, 112; of exclusion, 113, 115–16; negotiation of, 126; paradox of, 116–21
Iowa State University, 36
isolation, 39, 193

J
Jim Crow, 68
job dissatisfaction, 80
Johnson, Stephanie K., 196
Jordon, Jackson, 66

K
Kansas Board of Regents, 151–53
Kansas State University, 32
Kendi, Ibram X., 1
Kezar, Adrianna, 38, 141

Kokan, Zeba, 7, 189, 191, 192; positionality in racism study, 26–27; as Truman Scholar, 26
Kotter, John P., 2

L
Latinos, 31; visibility of, 117–19
Latinx, 7, 36, 102, 137; affinity space, 117–18; in DEI, 119; distinct history, experience, and needs, 190; identity, in PWIs, 113–16; stereotyping of, 114; university leadership, 188
leadership: behavioral theories of, 162; Black women and, 12–14, 58, 157–58, 165–67; Black women at HBCUs, 168–69; business approach to, 4; change and, 2; contingency theories of, 163; decision-making in, 200; defined, 162; diversity lacking in, 9; grassroots leaders, 139; in higher education, 162–65; new forms of, 198–99; power theories of, 163; Subramaniam and, 25; theories and models, 162–65; trait theories of, 162; women of color and, 2–4, 42, 126, 187; work of, 3, 188. *See also* disruptive leadership; faculty leadership, social justice and; transformational leadership; university leadership
Leading a Diversity Culture Shift in Higher Education (Chun and Evans), 2
Leading Change (Kotter), 2
learned behavior, 177
learning outcomes, 123
Leggett-Robinson, Pamela, 7, 189, 194
lesbian, gay, bisexual, transgender, queer (LGBTQ), 139

Lewis, John, 55, 194
LGBTQ. *See* lesbian, gay, bisexual, transgender, queer
LGBTQ-phobia, 139, 140
Light in the Dark/Luz en lo oscuro (Anzaldúa), 131
Lorde, Audre, 72

M

Mach Dubé, Christy, 197
macroaggresions, 39
macrolevel process, 1, 2, 121, 125, 127
Massachusetts Institute of Technology, 32
McKee, Kimberly D., 3–4
mentoring: need for, 193; by women of color, 8
microaggressions, 3, 10, 12, 22, 139; bias and, 64; harm from, 105; in higher education, 178; against women of color, 190
microlevel process, 1; in institutionalizing diversity, 106, 111, 126–27
Middle Passage, 68
minorities, 198; Asian Americans as model, 83; as college presidents, 169, 170; in higher education, 5. *See also specific minorities*
minority-serving institutions (MSIs), 168, 169
misfit methods, 13; Ahmed coining, 136; in faculty leadership and social justice, 134–38, 140–47; misfit models, 134
Montoya, Margaret, 94
Moore, Wendy L, 20
MSIs. *See* minority-serving institutions
multiculturalism, 131–32; in racism on university campuses study, 34

N

National Hispanic Heritage Month, 113–15
Native Americans, 31
nativism, 142
New Jersey Institute of Technology, 30
9/11 terrorist attacks, 153
nonproductive agents, 147–48
nontenure academic workforce, 175
normative masculinity, 1, 198

O

Oberlin College, 160
On Being Included (Ahmed), 2
"On the Pulse of Morning" (Angelou), 71
open-ended questions, 86
opportunity: equity, 179; hiring, 39; whiteness as disruption, 121–25
oppression, 18, 69, 95, 134, 187; history and reality of, 121, 124, 192; racism study addressing, 33
Oregon State University, 30
organizational catalysts, 139
outsider-within: Collins coining, 67; in deaning while Black, 67–70
overt bias, 193

P

paper trails, 11; diversity in, 21, 37
patriarchy, 166
Patton Stacey, 40, 63–64
pay gap, 197
pedagogy: culturally relevant, for advisement in SLACs, 87–90; decolonized, 87, 89, 93; inclusivity in, 175
persistence, 68, 144, 151; as advisement issue, 82; student persistence, 79, 82
plantation politics, 159

police brutality, 153
police-centric assertions, 36
positionality, 6–9, 191
Posselt, Julie R., 4
power, 191; hoarding of, 195; power gap, 197; power theories of leadership, 163; white power, 176
predominantly white institutions (PWIs), 5; Ahmed on guests in, 62–63; CDOs in, 99–100; collaboration in, 70; covert racism in, 159; deaning while Black in, 55; exclusion in, 158; faculty of color in, 56–57; Latinx in, 113–16; leadership in, 63, 67; multiple marginalities in, 188; people of color burdened in, 94; stereotyping in, 12–13, 81; tenure at, 169
Presumed Incompetent (Gutiérrez y Muhs), 2–3, 93
Princeton University, 34, 35
privilege, 19, 72; white privilege, 38, 65, 94, 132, 176
professorships, 159–60, 169
Proust, Marcel, 89
Puwar, Nirmal, 25
PWIs. *See* predominantly white institutions

Q

queer use: Ahmed on, 136–37, 149–51; in faculty leadership and social justice, 134–37, 147–51

R

race: aversion to talks of, 64–65; college presidents by, 171; course requirements for, 121–25, 193; racialized exclusion, 20–21
racial crises: recovery from, 41;

response of university leaders, 37–38, 41
racialization, 20, 122, 124
racial justice, 55, 68, 194; good necessary trouble for, 75; as marathon, 31; movements, 187; protests for, 200; in racism study, 32–33, 33; as unfinished business, 56
racism, 11, 124, 138; attacks, 142; avoidance of, 64; covert, in PWIs, 159; higher education and, 18; history of, 192; institutionalized racism, 81, 175; institutional whiteness veiling, 58; naming of, 21; response, in deaning while Black, 72; structural racism, 175; systemic, 2, 18, 58; university leaders and, 19–23. *See also* anti-racism
racism on university campuses study: alliances and solidarity addressed in, 30–33, 32, 37–39; anti-racism addressed in, 29, 31; author positionality in, 24–27; bias, 30; conclusion for university leadership, 36–42; COVID-19 pandemic addressed in, 32; DEI addressed in, 30, 33–36, 34; equality addressed in, 33–36, 34; Floyd death addressed in, 23, 29, 36; framework for, 19–23; justice addressed in, 32–33, 33; multiculturalism addressed in, 34; oppression addressed in, 33; police-centric assertions in, 36; profile of statements for, 27–36; racism and violence addressed, 28–30, 29; statement authors, 27, 28; statement data for, 23–24; statement list for, 42–49
recruitment: for advisement in SLACs, 92; of faculty of color, 63;

recruitment (*continued*)
  goals, for women of color, 191, 199; of students of color, 56, 63, 126; by university leadership, 39
reflective judgment, 177
reflexivity, 6–9
Reframing Academic Leadership (Bolman and Gallos), 2
Remembrance of Things Past (Proust), 89
resilience, 178; of women of color, 193
retention, 106; of faculty of color, 39; student retention, 84–85; of women of color, 191
Rethinking Diversity Frameworks (Chun and Feagin), 2
Roberts, Alberta, 66
role models: attracting, 195; Black women as, 179

S
Scott-Johnson, Pamela E., 7, 189, 194
scratched walls: Ahmed on, 135, 137–38; in faculty leadership and social justice, 134–39; of higher education, 13–14; numbers of, 193
second shift, 120
self-reflection, 177
Settles, I. H., 112
sexism, 11
sexual violence, 146
Shaw, Susan, 95
Silbert, Andrea, 197
situational awareness, 177
SLACs. *See* small liberal arts colleges
slavery, 68; wealth accrued from, 158
small liberal arts colleges (SLACs), 80; budget cuts in, 91; shortcomings of, 94. *See also* advisement in SLACs

social ingenuity, 175
social justice, 10, 179; commitment to, 59; deaning while Black and, 59, 69, 74; higher education and, 173; hitting brick walls in, 190; in racism study, 32–33, 33; task forces, 131–32. *See also* faculty leadership, social justice and
solidarity, 190, 191; building, 192; racism study addressing, 30–33, 32, 37–39
The Souls of Black Folk (Du Bois), 59–60
Squire, Dian, 159
stakeholder engagement, 177
stalking, 146
stereotyping, 3, 193; in advisement in SLACs, 84; Black women shattering, 169; gendered stereotypes, 187–88; of Latinx, 114; in PWIs, 12–13, 81; women of color experiences, 6–7
Stewart, Abigail J., 2, 141–42
Stewart, Davina-Lazarus, 74–75
storytelling, 87–88. *See also* counter-storytelling
Strategic Diversity Leadership (Williams), 2
strategic thinking, 178
stress, 80
structural racism, 175
students: Black women, 160; marginalized students, 80; student demographics, 173, 174, 175; student persistence, 79, 82; student retention, 84–85
students of color, 6, 40, 82, 190; advisors to, 8; experience of, 3–4; recruitment of, 56, 63, 126
Subramaniam, Mangala, 7, 9, 189, 191,

192; leadership and, 25; positionality in racism study, 24–26; on support from allies, 194
Susan Bulkeley Butler Center for Leadership Excellence, 25

T
Tamtik, Merli, 20–21
teacher burnout, 80
technical ingenuity, 175
tempered radicals, 139, 143
tenure: for Black women, 168–69; faculty leadership reaction to elimination, 152–53; for faculty of color, 85; at HBCUs, 169; nontenure academic workforce, 175; at PWIs, 169
theory of disruptive innovation, 164
tokenism, 3, 178; women of color experiences, 6–7
trait theories of leadership, 162
transformational leadership, 14, 200; defined, 163; disruptive leadership compared to, 177; intentionality in, 177; intersectionality and, 179; skills for, 177
translocal learning, 176
trust building, 106
Truth, Sojourner, 71
truth telling, 159
Truth Without Tears (Hodges and Welch), 3
Tubman, Harriet, 71

U
university leadership: African Americans, 188; alter of internal structures, 73; Asian Americans, 188; capacity-building and, 41; change in narrative of, 73; deconstructing diversity and inclusion,

74–75; diversity meaning and, 21–22; Hodges and Welch on top university leaders, 196–97; on inclusion, 40–41; Latinx, 188; preparation for, 104; in PWIs, 63, 67; racism and, 19–23; racism study and, 36–42; recruiting by, 39; response to racial crises, 37–38, 41; whiteness among, 20
University of California, Berkeley, 33
University of Kansas, 152
University of Michigan, 104
University of Mississippi, 34
University of Tennessee, 28

V
Valian, Virginia, 2, 141–42
violence, 11; African Americans impacted by, 187; dating violence, 146; domestic violence, 146; racism study addressing, 28–30, 29; sexual violence, 146
visibility, 112; in institutionalizing diversity, 113–16; of Latinos, 117–19
voices from periphery, 178, 188

W
Walcott, Rinaldo, 132–34, 148–49, 151, 154
Wambura Ngunjiri, Faith, 142–43
Washington, D. C. terrorist attack (2021), 152
Welch, Olga M., 3, 7, 8, 9–10, 189; on hiring agents of change, 194; on top university leaders, 196–97
wench in the works, 147–48
What's the Use? (Ahmed), 135
white fragility, 1, 65
White Fragility (DiAngelo), 1
white hegemony, 103, 168

white masculine norms, 109

whiteness, 198; Ahmed on responsibility for, 65; among university leaders, 20; disruption opportunities, 121–25; enduring whiteness of educational professionals, 57; perceptions of, 58; unmaking of, 132; unveiling lie of, 63–67. *See also* institutional whiteness

white power, 176

white privilege, 38, 65, 94, 132, 176

white supremacy, 22, 132, 138

"Why I Clap Back Against Racist Trolls Who Attack Black Women Academics" (Patton), 40, 63–64

Williams, Damon A., 2, 125

women of color: advocates for, 194; CDOs, 100; competence of, 196; counterstories, 200; cultural change propelled by, 193; deaning while Black by, 58; decision-making by, 193; earnings of, 189; exclusion and, 199; glass ceiling and, 58; in higher education administration, 5–6; hitting brick walls, 190; interactions with colleagues, 105; invisibility/hypervisibility of, 7–8; leadership and, 2–4, 42, 126; listening to, 196–97; men outnumbering in higher education, 57; mentoring by, 8; microaggressions against, 190; monitoring of, 10; recruitment goals for, 191, 199; resilience of, 193; retention goals for, 191; senior leadership and, 187; silence and, 198; stereotyping and tokenization experiences, 6–7; stories of, 71–72. *See also* African Americans; Asian Americans; faculty of color; Latinx

Y

Yakas, Laura, 134

CPSIA information can be obtained
at www.ICGtesting.com
Printed in the USA
LVHW081620130922
728178LV00002BA/397